HYPNO
for beginners
(easy techniques to learn hypnotism)

Prof. B.V. Pattabhi Ram

Director
Indian Institute of Clinical Hypnosis

PUSTAK MAHAL®

Publishers
Pustak Mahal®

J-3/16 , Daryaganj, New Delhi-110002
☎ 23276539, 23272783, 23272784 • *Fax:* 011-23260518
E-mail: info@pustakmahal.com • *Website:* www.pustakmahal.com

Sales Centre
■ 10-B, Netaji Subhash Marg, Daryaganj, New Delhi-110002
☎ 23268292, 23268293, 23279900 • *Fax:* 011-23280567
E-mail: rapidexdelhi@indiatimes.com
■ Hind Pustak Bhawan
6686, Khari Baoli, Delhi-110006
☎ 23944314, 23911979

Branches
Bengaluru: ☎ 080-22234025 • *Telefax:* 080-22240209
E-mail: pustak@airtelmail.in • pustak@sancharnet.in
Mumbai: ☎ 022-22010941, 022-22053387
E-mail: rapidex@bom5.vsnl.net.in
Patna: ☎ 0612-3294193 • *Telefax:* 0612-2302719
E-mail: rapidexptn@rediffmail.com
Hyderabad: *Telefax:* 040-24737290
E-mail: pustakmahalhyd@yahoo.co.in

© **Pustak Mahal, New Delhi**

ISBN 978-81-223-0429-9

Edition: 2010

The Copyright of this book, as well as all matter contained herein (including illustrations) rests with the Publishers. No person shall copy the name of the book, its title design, matter and illustrations in any form and in any language, totally or partially or in any distorted form. Anybody doing so shall face legal action and will be responsible for damages.

Printed at : Unique Color Carton, Delhi

Preface

Most of the Indians are not conscious about mental health and dental health. The reasons may vary from person to person. Now it is hightime to assess our personality, and we must learn techniques to convert our stress into relaxation. Here is an exclusive and lucid way to experience it. The aim of this book is twofold. First, it sets out to illustrate the range and diversity of scientific hypnotism for personal and professional reasons; second, it provides a substantial body of case material for the students of Psycho-pathology. All the cases in the book are real life examples selected from my works, but the names and places are not real.

Hypnosis as a phenomenon is now becoming well documented and more readily accepted. Unfortunately it is still clouded in mystery as far as the public at large is concerned. This arises partly out of sheer ignorance of fake hypnotists who do not have any basic knowledge about the science of behaviour. The chapters in this book were selected so as to represent the major areas with which an amateur hypnotist will need to be familiar in order to make the most of his upcoming counselling involvement. The chapters on the history of hypnotism, and development are intended to provide perspective on the field. There are variety of chapters dealing with study of behaviour, diagnosis assessment and testing which will enable the reader to evaluate the case. It is also obvious that although the material in this book was prepared primarily for psychologists, amateur hypnotists, mental health professionals in other disciplines, as well as there who wish to practice self hypnotism to overcome day to day tensions, stress, fatigue and anxiety.

Hypnosis, whether it is self-hypnosis or heterohypnosis is not a panacea-a cure for all diseases. It is not a means of becoming superhuman or a miracle man. It is simply a method of reaching your mind and marshalling the hidden talents, which most of us fail to tap, thus preventing ourselves from attaining our full potential. Hypnosis will not enable you to do something that you can't do, it can however, allow you to go beyond what you normally do, because you tap your inner reserves which are there. Hypnosis is now being used by doctors, anaesthetists, dentists and other therapists to help, cure or relieve a wide range of illnesses, personality disorders, emotional and psychological conditions. Now in Western countries, hypnosis is being used to treat people suffering from psychosomatic disorders, fears, phobias, to help people give up smoking, alcohol and drugs, to overcome shyness, stammering, nail biting, inferiority complex, tensions, impotency, frigidity and so on.

Finally I would like to express my sincere appreciation to Sri Pisapati Venugopal, Sri R.R. Rao, Shri Lakshmi Narasimharao who are loving and competent people right from 'conceiving' to its 'delivery', as book publication is as stressful as giving birth to a child. I'd like to express gratitude to Ms. Kaveribai for patiently typing my zigzag manuscript and to Shri B.V. Satya Nagesh, a well known psychologist.

I wish to record my thanks to M/s Pustak Mahal whose support and suggestions were instrumental in presenting this book.

B.V. Pattabhi Ram

Prasanthi
A-102, Venkata Ramana Apts,
A.C. Guards,
Hyderabad-500 004
Phone: 040-3396090/3327393

Contents ────────────

Hypnotism 1

Hypnotism is a splendid science. It has opened new vistas of knowledge to medicine. Medical experts have come to regard it as the most powerful method to treat mental illness. Intensive research has been carried out in this discipline over the past hundred years. Hypnotism is establishing itself more and more firmly as a valuable adjunct to traditional methods of diagnosing and treating psychological illnesses, and to eliminate unwanted social habits such as inferiority complex, smoking, overeating, postponement, irrational fears and phobias, addiction to alcohol, and drugs. Any one with an iota of interest can study this science and derive immense benefit with the help of an experienced hypnotist. As Milton rightly quoted in his *Paradise Lost*, "The mind in its own place, and it itself can make a heaven of hell, a hell of heaven". A person can give a negative or positive suggestion to his subconscious mind. The society in which we live bombards us continually with all types of suggestions and confuses the average man, leads him to fear, worry, anxiety, excitement, jealousy, anger, ego, inferiority complex and other psychological disturbances.

Unfortunately, in India we have terrible misconceptions about hypnosis. Many eyebrows are raised. Several suspicions are expressed. Many people are sceptical of the word hypnotism. They think it as a sham, fiction, black magic and illusion. Only unscrupulous persons, it is generally believed, practise hypnotism and allure people for their selfish ends. All these doubts are baseless. Unfortunately, it has often been connected with hoaxers,

Hypnos — the Greek God of Sleep

charlatans, second rate fiction and third rate film productions. It is all due to a lack of knowledge in the science of hypnotism.

The word "Hypnotism" is derived from the Greek word *Hypnos* which means "sleep". It is one of the most remarkable phenomena known to man. It is as old as the human mind, as aged as the world. It is a science of making a person to relax and enjoy trance like state known as hypnosis.

The Egyptians, Persians, Greeks and Romans were the first to recognise its power. The religious practices of certain oriental race often used the principles of hypnotism. The laying of hands on a diseased part of the body to bring a cure dates back to the time of the Bible. In the same way, the "Royal-touch" of the old King of France is reported to have effected many cures.

Hypnotism cured many people who became neurotic after the two World Wars. The anxieties, depressions, conflicts and fears that led to their break down were brought to surface. The entire field of psychotherapy has been greatly enriched by the application of hypnotism. Therefore, in 1956, the British Medical Association and in 1958, the American Medical Association approved and recognised officially the use of hypnotism in the medical field.

8

Hypnotism is defined as a mental state resembling a sleep like condition, which is induced by a suggestion of the hypnotist. The hypnotic state is similar to the state of mind prior to sleep. Every mentally healthy person is naturally susceptible and therefore hypnotisable. The ability of the person to concentrate his attention is the determining factor in the induction of the hypnosis. The most important factor is, gaining the attention of the person for the purpose of directing his thoughts so that they are focused on one single idea.

A trained hypnotist can help a mentally normal person to become a good hypnotic-subject, if he fails to go to sleep at the first attempt, it does not establish him as a poor hypnotic-subject. Hypnotist will have to try again. In fact the hypnotist is only a guide to make the subject to go into hypnotic sleep.

People who wish to be hypnotised and enjoy the state of relaxation, must understand three important points. Firstly, you should have a strong desire to get hypnotised without any reservation or resistance at any point. Secondly in the hypnotic state you do not become unconscious and will not do anything against your deep rooted principles. In the deepest hypnotic state you are awake and know what you are doing. Finally you don't need to have any "will-power" to enjoy the state of relaxation, as the commonly understood concept of "will-power" is a myth.

The Forerunners of Scientific Hypnotism

The ideas, theories and experiences of some famous physicians, neurologists and psychiatrists; who lived between early 17th century and beginning of 19th century are still considered as the basis of present days scientific studies on the subject of "Scientific Hypnotism."

The indepth studies on the subject made by the forerunners like Mesmer, Braid, Eliotson, Charcot and so on are briefly discussed in the following paragraphs.

9

Friedrich Anton Mesmer — The Propounder of Animal Magnetism

An Austrian physician Friedrich Anton Mesmer (1733-1815) of Vienna propounded the theory that a "Cosmic Fluid" could be stored in lifeless objects like magnets, and transferred to patients to cure them of their illness. Mesmer used to wear gorgeous dress. His consulting room was adorned with mirrors on all sides. It was dimly lit with waves of soft music flowing inside the room, into the deep silence and dull atmosphere.

Mesmer achieved his success when he treated a young lady Fraulein Oesterline, 29. She was suffering from a "Convulsive Malady" which was termed as "nervous disorder". Her symptoms consisted of blood rushing to head. She has terrible pain in her ears and head, followed by delirium, rage, vomiting and swooning. Mesmer applied three magnets to the patient's stomach and legs. She experienced a sensation all over her body followed by complete relief from her ailments.

Another way of curing that Mesmer adopted was, to make his patients sit in a circle round a large tub or tank containing powdered glass and iron filings. The patients held on to the iron rods, emerging from the tub. The rods were supposed to transmit the curative force to the patients.

Later on Mesmer discarded the magnets. He began to regard himself as a magnet with a fluid-life-force which could be transferred to others to heal their diseases. Mesmer called it "Animal Magnetism".

Occasionally Mesmer treated his patients with magnets also. Thousands of sick people with high hopes, thronged at his clinic. The patients were literally "mesmerized" to believe and expect that they would be cured. Consequently he earned name and fame by leaps and bounds and amassed wealth. He married an affluent widow and they purchased a beautiful mansion. He reached the zenith of his glory.

10

Mesmer fell into bad repute as a physician and magnetiser in Austria when he treated Marie Therese Parades, a pianist, who was blind since the age of four. In fact Mesmer had restored her eyesight. The physicians around him raised doubts about the reliability of his treatment. Marie Therese's father was Secretary to the Emperor and Empress. So he was afraid that some of the benefits which his daughter enjoyed as a blind lady might be withdrawn by the Government. So his attitude coupled with his skillful handling of the patient, Marie Therese, resulted in causing a setback to the fine treatment of Mesmer, the ablest physician known at the time. So, the blindness of the patient Marie Therese, relapsed. The frenzied outlook of the people around, at the turn of events paved the way for the exit of Mesmer from Paris in 1778 for good.

In France, Dr. Charles D'Eslen, a physician of repute, welcomed Mesmer with open arms. Mesmer soon became the passion of Paris. At a central place in his consulting room, a large tub or tank filled with water was placed from which metal bars were projected. His patients sat round the tub each holding one of the iron bars. Dr. Mesmer touched each one wielding an iron rod. Many of them fell with

Anton Mesmer's method of treatment

bizarre sensations. After two or three such sessions they felt cured.

Mesmer had maintained that he was harnessing the celestial force which flowed through his body to the iron rods and finally to the patients, to restore their natural health. Further he contended that he could get the electrical force in his body without the aid of the magnetic rods. The physicians of France were envy of the popularity and reputation of Mesmer. They raised hue and cry against his system with the result that in 1784, King Louis XVI set up a Royal Commission which included such giants as Benjamin Franklin, a noted Scientist and Writer, Dr. Joseph Guillotine who invented the beheading instrument and Antoine Lavoisier, a Scientist and the discoverer of Oxygen.

The Commission concluded that the cures could be explained only by the imagination of the subject. The report was not comprehensive. It did not mention the positive results of Mesmer's stupendous work, the psychological implications of the illnesses and the results of his treatment. The Commission has not understood that the cure was genuine even when there was no physical or organic origin to the illness. Mesmer was condemned by the Royal Decree.

Undaunted by the Commission's report, Mesmer refused to renounce his cherished beliefs. He left France for Meersburg where he expired on 5th March 1815. But his name became immortal and rendered him a legendary figure in the history of psychotherapy. He was an early experimenter in hypnosis, which was formerly and popularly called "mesmerism" after his name.

Dr. James Braid — The First Student of Real Scientific Hypnotism

The concept of mesmerism led to new ideas and theories. An English Physician, Dr. James Braid (1795-1860) gave mesmerism a scientific perspective. He considered mesmerism as a nervous sleep and coined the word "HYPNOSIS" derived from the Greek word "HYPNO" meaning sleep. Braid showed that hypnotised subjects were often abnormally susceptible and sensitive to impressions on the senses and that much of the subject's behaviour was the result of the suggestions given verbally.

Once Dr. Braid happened to attend a stage show in London by one Lappentine of France who was a Magician-cum-Hypnotist. During the course of the magic show the hypnotist made his subject seated on a chair, pierced him with needles, made peculiar sounds resembling those of wailing wolves near his ear and made him drink a bitter medicinal juice. In spite of all this the subject was unperturbed and remained calm. There was no feeling of fear or any of that sort in his face. Dr. Braid thought that the magician was deceiving. After returning home he made one of his patients sit on a chair and gave some suggestions to him. He was stunned and embarrassed. It was almost a repeat performance. Later he acquired a good number of books on mesmerism and took interest in the subject with faith and propagated the mesmeric cult.

Negative mental attitude killing by giving suggestion

The police officials of that period, while criticising the methods of Braid, followed his system in a different way. Braid treated his patients by his system of suggestion and cured them of their ailments, whereas the police officials went a step further and rendered

13

healthy person weary, desolate and finally succumb to their pranks.

Their *modus operandi* was startling. Once in Copenhagen they imprisoned a person accused of a murder. They blindfolded him and told him that they would prick his body with needles till he died. Then they opened behind him a water tap from which water trickled down drop by drop. The prisoner felt that his blood was oozing out of his body and so started feeling weak. The police officers again suggested to him that he lost much blood and he would die within ten minutes. The accused took the "suggestion" seriously and expired in seven minutes. Braid detested such perverted methods of the police in punishing the accused.

Dr. Braid paved the way for extending medical facility by means of hypnotism to cure diseases and he called this new concept as "Hypnotherapy", also known as hypnosis.

So, as stated earlier, hypnosis is a sleep like condition psychically induced usually by another person, in which the subject is in a state of altered consciousness and responds with certain limitations to the suggestions of the hypnotist.

Dr. James Braid died in 1860. Sigmond Freud, the great inventor of psychoanalysis stated in clear terms that Dr. James Braid could be regarded as the first student of real scientific hypnotism.

John Elliotson —
The Explorer of Mysteries in Human Mind

Mention may be made here of some of the applications of hypnosis. Elliotson was a friend of the noted painter and illustrator Cruikshank and also the famous British novelist, W.M. Thackeray. He was also a contemporary of the poet Keats.

Elliotson was appointed as an assistant physician at St. Thomas's Hospital on 17th October 1817. He was elected

Professor of medicine in 1831. Three years later the North London Hospital was opened and Elliotson became its physician. In 1837, it was upgraded to University level. Elliotson believed that the medical students should be taught at the bed side rather than by serving for five years as apprentice to a senior doctor. At that time, the operations were conducted without anaesthesia, and psychological medicine was still in its infancy. He was inspired to explore the mysteries of the human mind.

Medical history has many innovations initiated by Elliotson. He was one of the first to use the stethoscope and taught how to examine the chest. He made many discoveries and valuable observations on the use of drugs. He gave the highly enlightening lectures at the Royal College of Physicians in 1829 on "The Art of differentiating various diseases of the heart", and his notes on the *"Theory and Practice of Medicine"* were great contributions to medical treatment. Elliotson had declared that animal magnetism was effected by uniting the will of the patient with that of the doctor. The patient exhibited physical convulsions and passed into the mesmeric trance in which state he could be cured of his illness. Elliotson started a journal called *The Zoist*. It was mainly concerned with mesmerism and numerous cases of treatment were reported.

In those days, Mesmerism was the only form of anaesthesia available before ether was introduced by Morton in 1846 and chloroform by Simpson in 1847. A Scottish Surgeon, James Esdoils (1808-1859) who was working in Calcutta, had performed many painless operations like the amputation of limbs, using mesmerism which he called "magnetic sleep", created sensation in the field of medicine.

Jean Martin Charcot— The Neurologist of a Different Technique

Jean Martin Charcot, 1825-1893 a neurologist in Paris explained hypnosis as a state of abnormal neurological activity.

Charcot demonstrating Hypnotism technique

The newly wed women have little interest in sex and sometimes show a negative attitude towards it. In all sex problems, basically there is inhibition, frigidity, confusion, faulty thinking and fear. Feelings of inferiority and insecurity are very common. A wrong notion of the men that they are impotent may blur the relationship with their wives. Dr. Jean Charcot made use of the hypnotism technique and brought relief to many couples and there was all round happiness.

Sigmund Freud, the great inventor of Psychoanalysis accepted that our neurosis or nervous habits are buried in the unconscious and that therein lies the origin of subsequent neurotic illness. It could be said to be the direct result of Elliotson's work. Sigmund Freud while supporting the treatment of Charcot in relieving the patients of their diseases, compared the hypnotic state with that of being in love. Hypnosis, he said, was a very particular form of relationship. He maintained that if psychotherapy was ever to become widely available to the public, the use of hypnosis as a shortcut procedure would be essential. Whenever a patient visited Freud for treatment, by his "Free Association" method he created a congenial atmosphere for the patient and conducted treatment with palatable words. Freud explained the efficacy of his treatment by writing articles in German language, while experts and psychologists extended their unstinted support to Freudian theories and brought relief to the suffering multitude later on.

In France, August Ambroise Liebeault (1823-1904) and Hippolyte Bernheim (1837-1919) were the supporters of hypnosis. They regarded hypnosis as a normal phenomenon. They asserted that imagination was the most important factor in the induction of hypnosis, that increased suggestibility was its essential symptom, and that the hypnotist worked on the patient by mental influences. They propagated their cult through "Nancy School of Hypnotism". The frigidity of woman, the feelings of impotency, inferiority, somnambulism, insomnia, loss of self confidence, amnesia, fears and phobias had all been treated by the doctors of Nancy School of Hypnotism.

Franklin Roosevelt, the former President of the U.S.A., noted for his intellect, was a strong supporter of hypnotism. Roosevelt opined that hypnotism improved one's confidence to achieve the cherished goals in time, "is one's jewel".

Hypnotism stood the test of time and blossomed into a valuable science, like gold withstanding the heat of oven, before being transformed into a glittering jewel.

When doctors, medical scientists and intelligentsia were playing an important role in extending their support to hypnotic cult and hypnotherapy, the activities of pseudo hypnotists brought discomfort to genuine practitioners whose main concern was to bring relief to those who were affected with psychosomatic disorders. The fake hypnotists cared more for cheap popularity and pecuniary gain through questionable methods. Those hypnotists and their liberal payments to persons who helped them in such shows were detected by the police in Texas. Their *modus operandi* was exposed. The police nabbed such pseudo hypnotists and prosecuted them.

Anton Mesmer at work with magnetized water

Nevertheless, the interest of people continued and they invited the genuine hypnotists to their villages and cities, assimilated the essence of their talk, and came forward to be treated through hypnotherapy. Exposure of the shady activities of pseudo hypnotists reinforced the interest of the people in hypnotic cult. Unstinted support and encouragement of the people brought a new glory to the efforts of real hypnotists to popularise their system of treatment in relieving the patients of their ailments.

■ ■

Hypnotism: Recognition by Government

After facing much furore and criticism, hypnotism got its place of pride firmly with the determined support of intellectuals and medical professionals. The medical journals and popular magazines extended their support and finally hypnotic treatment was recognised the world over. The British government gave its assent to Hypnotism Act in 1952. The subject of hypnotherapy became a part of the Act and hence it was included in the medical jurisprudence.

In order to curtail the activities of pseudo hypnotists, Clause 2 (1) stipulates that hypnotism shows should not be conducted in public places, at any gathering where persons have assembled or at any dance or music concerts, or at any sports event, pastime and interesting pursuit. If any one contravenes this clause, he shall be considered a criminal and he could be liable to prosecution.

The American government also extended its support to hypnotism by providing many facilities to medical practitioners and medical specialists who practised hypnotherapy and encouraged further research in it. The result being many hypnotists and hypnotherapists have been practising since then, in every suburb and city of America.

Statistics show that twenty to thirty thousand women in America have gone through painless delivery under hypnosis. In addition, there have been thousands of others who had therapeutic treatment in which hypnotic techniques were used. The

Extracting a tooth through hypnosis

gynaecologists and dentists deserve special mention here for they used hypnosis during their treatment in several cases.

In a well known study by Davidson published in the British Medical Journal, the duration of labour was considerably reduced for the seventy patients treated by hypnosis, and nearly sixty percent needed no analgesics. It is also interesting to note that studies in U.S.A. had shown that babies born under hypnosis were in a much better condition than those delivered with the help of nurses. The gynaecologists made the delivery of a child a painless experience and it was considered a pleasant experience. A book titled *Painless Delivery Through Hypnotism* was well received by the people and nearly three lakh copies were sold as hot cakes which testified the popularity of the treatment. Some dental-hypnotherapists maintain that the mouth is a very special cavity in the Freudian sense, it is associated with some very exclusive problems, and so hypnotherapy is very useful in dentistry to the patients who are trained in auto-hypnosis or the ability to go into hypnotic trance at a signal. The relaxation technique can be applied to adults and children by the dentist to derive much benefit. Usually children are not only highly anxious patients, but fortunately they are also good hypnotic subjects. A dentist trained in hypnosis can extract teeth of his patients quite painlessly.

The psychiatrists brought relief with the help of hypnotherapy to those patients suffering from sleeplessness, somnambulism, nail biting, inferiority complex, fears, phobias and lack of self confidence. Equally surprising, the dermatologists treated their patients by hypnotherapy in minimising and controlling their morbid skin diseases like warts etc.

The dedicated and genuine hypnotists were emboldened to organise scientific hypnotic shows freely with the support of authorities.

Is there any relationship between Magic and Hypnotism?

Usually some magicians organise hypnotic shows too. It has become a fashion. There is a reason for that. In the earlier times young men and women were trained in magic by Royal College of London. Along with magic the lecturers taught them other subjects like physics, chemistry, electricity and also hypnotism to improve their self confidence. So those magicians who mastered hypnotism included it as one of the items in their shows.

Strictly speaking there is no relationship between hypnotism and magic. Magic is an art whereas hypnotism is a science. Every magician must have self confidence to practise magic or for conducting magic shows. So, a magician has to learn hypnotism. But there is no such need for a hypnotist to try a hand at magic.

Following this, magicians the world over were devoted to the subject of hypnotism and arranged stage shows to the satisfaction of the audience. John Arwell, Peter Fernandez of U.S.A., Cleave Chesterfield of England and Amazing Brooklyn of Australia were the most reputed magicians of that era. But at the same time people should not view that every magician is adept in hypnotism also. It is a misconceived notion. Among our Indian magicians, there is a tendency to boast of their skill in hypnotism. They project such false image just to create an aura of expertise. When I recently visited Udaipur to participate in an All India Magicians Seminar, I have come across such magicians. I have arranged scientific hypnotic shows for their benefit for a period of five days, to help them to become genuine hypnotists.

The subject of hypnotism is a marvellous one. It has astonishing power in it. Any avid artist can learn, practise and exhibit it. But they are not fit to mitigate the suffering of ailing patients by using their gestures, etc.

The tribe of stage hypnotists in our country should grow. The newspapers and the media have been extending their unstinted support to the subject of hypnotism. The people are now inclined to it and encouraging it in a generous way. If the present trend continues, the State government and the Central government can mobilise all assistance and support needed for Scientific Hypnotism to put it on an even keel. I have tried in this book to

The author and his hypnotic subjects of Nigeria

22

convey the elementary knowledge of scientific hypnotism to the learners. During early eighties I visited U.S.A., Canada, Malaysia, Singapore, Nigeria, Arab countries and Thailand and obtained first hand information on the progress made till now. My experience with some hypnotists of repute in these countries is included in this book.

Those who study this book, can become fine hypnotists. They gain self-confidence to serve the Society. The one who learnt the essentials of psychology can serve the society in a better way.

The medical students, the psychologists, and the psychiatrists can make good use of the experiences mentioned in this book and enrich their expertise.

Ten Commandments

Like the Ten Commandments enshrined in the Holy Bible, the prospective hypnotist should master ten important points. The present day hypnotist is expected to have mastered these ten important points to reach the pinnacle.

1. The hypnotist should be well versed in his subject. He should be able to answer any question on the subject. After taking the consent of the patient, the hypnotist has to make his suggestions to him as per detailed instructions agreed upon earlier.

2. The person who is to be hypnotised is called the "subject". The subject should be seated in a chair comfortably and the hypnotist should make a suggestion in a language familiar to the subject to close his eyes. The presence of interpreters or translators is unnecessary when there is a clear rapport between the hypnotist and his subject.

3. The suggestions should be simple and direct. The suggestion should be given in a soothing manner. If the voice of the hypnotist is vehement or a bit commanding, then the subject

23

may not go into a hypnotic state.

4. The language of suggestion should be simple with short sentences. The hypnotist may be a linguist. He might have mastered many languages. But he should not use difficult words and lengthy sentences. Then the subject may feel averse and loose interest in the hypnotic process itself. Easy and understandable language should be used by the hypnotist or therapist as the case may be.

5. It may be your first attempt or experiment to hypnotise the subject. You should not reveal it and request your subject to cooperate with you to follow your suggestions. If you plead so, the subject may get terrified and may not be hypnotised at all for reasons best known to him. You will come to know whether the subject has entered the hypnotic trance or not as your experience grows when you gain perfection in the art in due course of time.

6. Suggestions should be given directly in a firm but polite tone. Indirect suggestions may lead to complications.

7. When the subject while in trance is following the suggestions in letter and spirit, the hypnotist should not view the subject as a slave. If the subject feels anything averse from the side of the hypnotist, it will hurt his self respect and he will come out of the trance. Such situations were recorded when a woman subject was hypnotised with the idea of molesting her by a fake hypnotist.

8. Hypnotist should not commit mistakes while giving suggestions. You have to note down all the necessary and relevant suggestions on a paper and address these suggestions in a firm tone to the subject, as the subject would be following and adhering to all your suggestions with due care. While giving suggestions to the subject, the hypnotist should not swerve, deviate or commit mistakes.

9. When the subject is in the hypnotic trance, the hypnotist

should give a single pointed suggestion. Too many suggestions to cure all his ailments, some times bring adverse reactions.

10. At the end of the session, the subject should open his eyes with the conviction that a positive step is taken to cure his illness.

If the induction has been initiated by counting, say one to five, then awakening should be suggested by the reverse procedure of counting down from five to one.

Immediately following this, a suggestion should be given to the subject that he will begin to feel better, the hypnotic experience has been a learning experience and has shown him what he can accomplish in daily life. He should be told that on opening his eyes he will be alert and awake and ready to undertake whatever activity he wishes to do during the rest of the day, and he will remain calm and relaxed while doing so.

Hypnotism — Its Existence, State and Condition

The science of hypnotism is so vast that one has to study and digest it in a progressive way to appreciate its utility in mitigating the different psychological problems which human beings face during the course of their busy lives.

Before hypnotising a person the hypnotist should explain briefly about the treatment to him or her and clear doubts, if any. This is especially important in the case of Indian women who usually are afraid of hypnotism. It is the duty of the hypnotist to assure such women, that nothing would happen against their will, and they can be rest assured of good results and would feel happy and relaxed after the treatment.

Those subjects who are not at all willing to be hypnotised

should be avoided by the hypnotist. Under any circumstances, one should never attempt to hypnotise any one suffering from epilepsy or hysteria, unless the hypnotist has considerable knowledge of psychology. Therefore, before visiting a hypnotherapist one should find out whether the therapist has any knowledge of psychology or not.

Above all a good rapport is to be established with the subject. It will help to penetrate deep into the subconscious and provide a clear area for rebuilding healthier responses. A deep rapport gives invaluable support in the treatment of neurotic illnesses.

Finally, most of the patients entertain misconceptions and preconceived notions about hypnosis, the hypnotist has to eliminate them. Preconditioning, preparation and explanation should establish sufficient rapport and confidence to allow the patient to lower his defence. The subject must be made to understand that he or she will experience an unique, relaxing and refreshing form of therapy in which deep inner knowledge is the keynote to happiness.

■ ■

Levels of Hypnosis 3

Hypnosis is a peculiar state slightly different from the usual or normal awareness but not so different that it is immediately identifiable as such. There are three main stages or levels of hypnosis. They are Lethargic, Hallucinatory, and Somnambulistic states.

Lethargic State (Light Hypnotic State)

Lethargy means heavy unnatural slumber and dullness. Let us first imagine that the patient is lying on the bed. The initial introductory procedure has been concluded and the subject's eyes are closed. The room is quiet, the patient is comfortable. Nothing is heard except the soothing voice of the therapist. He is in the first or hypnoidal state. From his physical point of view, the subject appears to be completely comfortable but obviously aware of his surroundings. Although his eyes are closed and he appears to be in a completely relaxed state, you are aware that he can very easily be roused. He is certainly not yet ready for treatment and if woken up at this point he would say that he was drowsing but could wake up at that time.

Further suggestions of mental and physical relaxation are given and the hypoidal stage gradually deepens to the light trance state of hypnosis. The patient may be given reassuring suggestions. His problems can be discussed. He can be allowed to ventilate his feelings. He can recall memories of past events with greater ease. He can easily imagine situations suggested to him although his visualisation of such events need not necessarily

27

be realistic. As if cajoling a child, the therapist has to soothingly suggest to the patient so that the subject can enter the second state of hallucination.

Hallucinatory State (Medium Hypnotic State)

The word hallucination implies the apparent perception in a nervous or mental disorder of something external that is actually not present. It also occurs in some mental disorders. In general, the patient enters this stage from the lethargic state (first state) in nearly ten minutes depending upon their receptivity. In some cases due to the confidence and close association with their hypnotist the subject may directly enter this second stage very easily. When I was giving stage performance some of my subjects even in their first hypnotic experience entered this stage several times.

However, if relaxation continues, the patient passes into a deeper state in which he visualises suggested scenes (like Taj Mahal etc.), situations and sensations in a more realistic manner. The patient may also accept suggestions of amnesia (forgetting).

Stage hypnotism — Hallucinatory state

28

Another suggestion which may be given to the patient is that he is unable to open his eyes. As the patient attempts to do so, he passes into a deeper and deeper state of hypnosis. This is known as eye lid catalepsy (rigidity). Hallucination also means delusion. During the course of this hallucinatory state, if the therapist suggests to his subject, "You are now travelling in a car. You are driving your own car all by yourself. You can drive very well. So you are driving the car very very fast". On hearing this the subject feels that he is actually driving the car himself. So the therapists or the hypnotists should give to their subjects only those suggestions which are acceptable to them in all respects, instead of a suggestion that they are piloting an aeroplane or driving a car in which they don't have proficiency.

Somnambulistic State (Deep Hypnotic State)

The state in which the subject could open his eyes, talk, obey instructions and yet remain in hypnosis, was discovered by Marquise Puysegur a disciple of Mesmer. It was given the name "Somnambulism" from the two Latin words *somnus* meaning sleep and *ambulare* meaning walk. Those who can reach that state are known as Somnambulists. It is a state which is rarely required for treatment. Although its achievement may give a great deal of satisfaction to the therapist, it may result in bewilderment for the subject. The fact that many people are unable to achieve this level of depth does not in any way prevent from treatment, since medium or even light trance is often sufficient. Some therapists even maintain that it is sufficient to begin treatment if the patient closes his eyes and reaches a state somewhere between hypnoidal and light trance. This must depend, of course, on the seriousness of the problem and it should certainly be deep enough in some cases. A typical example of the somnambule is the person who is selected by the stage hypnotist to perform various contortions and obey his commands for the amusement of the audience.

Stage hypnotism — Somnambulistic state

A somnambulist who is amnesic can usually dissociate to a very high degree. But once again varying degree of dissociation can occur without amnesia. Dissociation, therefore, is neither necessary nor sufficient for hypnosis to occur.

Freud saw human personality in three inter-related systems and he called them "*Id*". It's the original source of personality with which a child is born including its instincts and drives. The "Id" works according to the "pleasure principle", it avoids pain and obtains pleasure, regardless of external considerations. The "Id" however, is constrained by the later developments of the "ego" and the "superego". The ego relates to the mental images with reality, it works according to the "reality principle" which requires it to test reality and delay any bodily tensions until the appropriate environment conditions are obtained.

The "ego" is realistic and logical, and its purpose is to create a plan which can be executed in the environment in which it lives, in order to achieve satisfaction. Thus the *Id* requires immediate satisfaction, which the *ego* intervenes and chooses the time, place and conditions. The *ego* is the "executor" of the *Id*.

The "superego" is concerned with a person's values and morals. As already stated the *ego* is the executor of the *Id*. The *superego* considers whether the plan of action, chosen by the ego does not violate the values and morals of the society to which the individual belongs.

It is very important to realise that when hypnosis is induced, we establish a direct link with the Id. But the superego is still operating at all times both in the waking and the hypnotic states. Because reality-testing has been suspended, the belief that a person can be fooled into believing something which is harmful is incorrect. If the superego is fooled, then the person may carry out something which the superego would normally have not allowed. For this to occur, the person would have to be a somnambulist so that the ego is fully suppressed. Further, this feeling of the ego can only take place in heterohypnosis, i.e., if you are hypnotising yourself you would not want to feel your superego.

In the deepest state of hypnosis, that is somnambulistic state, a person carries out all suggestions but is usually unaware of doing so. Now, how do we explain this phenomenon? In this state the left brain totally goes to sleep. Words, pass directly through the corpus callosum and into the right brain. Then the person usually acts literally according to the suggestions. Only about 50% of the subjects can achieve somnambulistic state. While in self hypnosis this will seldom occur because in such a state you may become incapable of giving yourself any further suggestion. If it does occur, then you will literally fall asleep and wake up at your convenient time like falling asleep in the chair while watching a television.

It was Puysegur who discovered somnambulism as a new dimension of magnetism, a state in which subjects could open their eyes, talk, obey instructions and yet remain 'magnetised'. The somnambulistic subjects were thought to be endowed with particular powers of prophecy and of diagnosis and their employment for the latter purposes became a fashionable and profitable venture. Under the influence of Puysegur, the unlimited enthusiasm of the magnetizer once again earned the antagonism of orthodox medicine. The biography of Edger Cayce (*There is a river by Thomas Shungro*) is worth quoting in this context.

Under somnambulistic state, the highly receptive state of the patient's mind yields good results. Elliotson had stated that 'wounds do not pain' and certain diseases could be cured under this state. Elliotson used this state on some of the patients for the purpose of diagnosis.

In 1957 and 1960 Professor Barry Wyke, a neurological scientist at Royal College of Surgeons in London pointed out that brain waves of the hypnotised person are similar to those produced by that person if he were awake but relaxed. The brain waves only change when sleep is deliberately and specifically induced by the hypnotist.

Accordingly it could be concluded that the deeply hypnotised person i.e. one who carried out all the suggestions given by the hypnotist and produces all the phenomena known in the somnambulistic state, is neither asleep nor awake in the accepted sense, but is in a very special state of relaxation. Hypnosis and sleep are distinct states. While the subject is in the hypnotic state he may also be suggested to fall asleep.

Some further studies were carried out by Regnoc Aladjalova and Kamenetsky of Russia and the findings were presented at the Seventh Industrial Congress of Hypnosis and Psychosomatic medicine held in Philadelphia in 1976. They confirmed that hypnosis was a special state which differed from that of either sleeping or waking. Further data obtained suggests that as hypnosis deepens at the somnambulistic level, the changes also become noticeable in the electrical activity of the brain. Changes also occur during hallucinated experiences. For example, if it is suggested that the subject can smell the scent of a rose, there is a definite alteration of electrical activity in the brain. In the waking state no such change is noticed when subjects are actually presented with a strong smelling substance. These Russian workers confirmed that there is a definite alteration in both the psychological and the physical states in hypnosis, a special state which differs from both sleep and wakefulness.

A particularly interesting case of an ex-British paratrooper shot down over Germany during the Second World War, may be recalled here. Let us call him Sergeant "A". This man subsequently developed a very severe neurosis and was subject to repeated attacks of extreme agitation. He had been given a considerable amount of medical treatment but to no avail and he had agreed to go through hypnotic treatment. During the induction period, he clearly demonstrated some of the attributes of the somnambule and it was decided to treat him by hypnotic regression and to allow him to ventilate his experiences and feelings.

At this state, he began to talk of the terrifying experience of his jump and descent amidst the hail of flak and machine gun fire. In the war front Sergeant "A" developed symptoms of battle fatigue and was transferred to another unit. He was emotionally distressed by the suffering that he saw around him and he broke down again. The threshold of his anxiety had been reached and symptoms of acute agitation developed.

He was ultimately discharged from the services and he returned to civil life, only to break down every time he reached this level of anxiety. Eventually his condition became chronic and he sought the help of a psychiatrist. While under hypnosis, recounting those war experiences, Sergeant "A" became very restless and agitated and he started re-living all these happenings in the true sense of "Freudian Catharsis". He was told to forget that in trance. Some time after this treatment was successfully concluded, his case was discussed at a clinical meeting held by members of a learned society. Sergeant "A" was only too happy

33

to attend and to answer questions after the discussion. "what did you feel like?" asked one member of the audience, "when you were recounting experiences whilst dropping over Germany and during the subsequent unpleasant adventures?" The sergeant looked puzzled for a moment and then said "I can't remember because the doctor told me to forget".

This case very clearly describes the enormous value of the use of amnesia in any successful hypnotherapeutic treatment.

As the hypnotic sessions are repeated, patients gain more confidence in themselves and in the therapy. The self imposed restrictions will begin to diminish and the patient eventually experiences deep trance. Nevertheless, it must be emphasised that each treatment must be tailored to suit the particular case, not the case to the treatment. If this is kept in mind, then most of the patients would respond positively.

In the case of dental patients, the patient is told that normal sensation will return when treatment is completed. While the subject is in deep trance and certainly in the somnambule, the analgesia can be produced by suggestion, directly on to the gum, and this procedure may be sufficient even for dental extractions. A good hypnotic subject can often be taught to produce analgesia thus saving quite a considerable amount of time.

■ ■

Neurosis 4

Since Freudian times, we have distinguished between the conscious mind and the unconscious mind. As generally understood the conscious brain is located in the left hemisphere of the brain, while the unconscious mind is located in the right hemisphere.

Franz Joseph Gall, a Viennese physician, the founder of the study of phrenology, claimed that mental development could be measured by the examination of the skull. Gall was a great student of the mind and maintained that emotions acted independently of the will and that this often resulted in physical effects. We may read in this the anticipation of the discovery of the unconscious mind, the later acceptance by Freud that our neuroses or nervous habits are buried in the unconscious mind and that therein lies the origins of subsequent neurotic illness. This could be the direct result of Elliotson's work.

Neurosis can be any of the various physical or mental functional disorders characterised by one or several of the following reactions viz., anxiety convulsions, obsessions, phobias, depressions and convulsions. Neurosis means suffering from nervous disorder. A neurotic person is an abnormally sensitive one.

Hypnosis is a particular state of mind. A hypnotised person is fully awake as shown by the brain wave pattern of Electro-Encephalo Graph (EEG). Yet from outward appearance he looks as if sleeping. In fact, hypnosis and sleep are quite different. The similarity is purely superficial. Though the word "hypnosis" is derived from a Greek word meaning sleep, this is purely etymological. Even so, as we shall see, the association of sleep with certain bodily changes is often utilized in hypnotic routines.

What are the correct indications for employing hypnotic therapy? Generally speaking, it should be applied only for the modification of a type of behaviour known as 'neurotic'. This word in every day usage may be offensive and derogatory. In no way this interpretation is implied in psychiatric language. Neurotic symptoms are nervous symptoms. A neurotic person is referred to one who is prone to nervous disorders.

A disorder of the nervous system produces certain recognized and diagnosable mental and physical signs and syndrome. It is a disorder characterised by one's inability to cope with the stresses of life, with relationships, a type of disorder which often results in mental conflict and, as in any other conflict, the consequence is that somebody gets hurt. In the case of a neurosis it is the patient who suffers the trauma with far reaching effects.

Erwin Stengel (1902-1973), a Viennese Psychiatrist, came to the United Kingdom in 1938 and held several important posts in England and Scotland. He was a man of considerable knowledge and experience. From 1956 he was Professor of Psychiatry at the University of Sheffield. He stated that one-third to one-tenth of the population is estimated to be suffering from mental disorders, and classified them as:

1. The neurosis in which there is usually no serious break with reality.

2. The psychosis in which patients suffer serious disturbance and a break with reality.

3. The mentally subnormal or deficient, that is, those with retarded intellectual development.

4. Those who have psychopathic personalities and show abnormally aggressive and irresponsible conduct.

In the treatment of such disorders, certainly hypnotherapy has an important role to play.

If we further examine the problems associated with the neurosis, a formidable array of symptoms become apparent giving rise to a large number of well known illnesses. Each of them in turn may appear as a specific problem or a combination of some other symptoms of neurosis. These may be listed as follows:

The Neurosis

- Anxiety,
- Psychosomatic illnessess (which cause mental problems),
- Aggression (of certain bodily responses),
- Phobias (irrational fears),
- Obsessions (compulsions),
- Hysterical symptoms (commonly a 'convulsion' of the anxiety to a physical symptom),
- Fatigue state (loss of memory or amnesia)

Problems of Personality

- Inferiority complex/superiority complex,
- Social disabilities (stammering, blushing, certain nervous habit - spasm ortics),
- Addictions (smoking, alcohol, drugs),
- Eating problems associated with body image (over eating and anorexia),
- Immature personalities,
- Psychosexual problems,
- Impotency,
- Frigidity,
- Some sexual variations, incest,
- Reactive depression,
- Hypochondriacis.

It should not be thought that the use of hypnosis is restricted entirely to the treatment of these specific neuroses. A large number of additional applications, (many of which may be associated with anxiety) also present ideal situations for treatment by this method. Some of these occur in dentistry, gynaecology, obstetrics, pain relief, sleep problems, etc. The use of hypnosis in the detection of crime is found to be extremely useful.

When the Second World War broke out, many people were frightened because of War, which turned them sick. The doctors alleviated their fear and suffering by means of hypnotherapy. As a matter of fact bright days began for hypnotherapeutic treatment since then. The physicians and psychologists started evincing keen interest in this subject. It established the fact that neurotic ailments could be cured by hypnotism, beyond doubt.

Neurosis is a kind of mental disease. It is a suffering from nervous disorder. Very few of such patients enter hospital for relief. This disease is not at all dangerous as some believe and it may not cause even noticeable physical harm. But such neurotic patients cannot remain happy or cheerful in the company of others. As they discharge their daily duties and social obligations in a routine manner, the people around them cannot recognise them as neurotic patients. But their habit and ideas differ from those of others in their company.

The neurotic patients lack mental peace. They brood over something which causes physical uneasiness and ill health. They view it as only a physical ailment and not at all a mental one. As per the statistics of the psychologists, one in every ten is a neurotic in our country. But this figure is much greater in countries like U.S.A., U.K. and Germany.

The intellectuals are of the opinion that anxiety, fear and selfishness of a person gives rise to conflict and these convert him into a neurotic. The neurotic cannot face the mental aberration that is taking place in his mind. He cannot make a compromise

38

with his opponents and because of fears and phobias, he loses self confidence and is mentally depressed. His aversion to do things, his blaming of others for his own failures, brings self to his "*Soma*". This leads to insomnia and anorexia. He becomes weak, enervated and sick.

Generally a person is vulnerable to neurosis due to the following bio-causes:

1. The genealogical history,

2. The events or situations prevailing at the time of the birth of the child or during childhood days,

3. The circumstances prevalent in the neighbourhood or in a town, a village or a city as the case may be,

4. The events or occurrences that take place in a society where the individual lives or habitate, and the environmental (social) factors.

The Genealogical History

Usually some people are apprehensive by attitude. Even a small trivial event may have a shattering impression on them and they radiate the same to people all around and near and dear is no exception. In their forlorn imagination they feel that their children also must be inheriting this apprehensive attitude. It need not necessarily be true. In some cases, it is well known to science that this fear psychosis causes diseases viz., skin ailments, stammering, natural micturition, etc. By so doing they unnecessarily incur the displeasure of others which forms part of their daily routine. They feel elated when others praise them and get depressed when they are chided. Such extreme feelings can be cured by hypnotherapy and this has already been proved by well known hypnotherapists of the world. In our Institute of Clinical Hypnosis, we have cured hundred of neurotic patients.

I know an elderly gentleman having three sons. He used to chide his sons while teaching them at home thus, "If you are not going to study properly, you are destined to become rickshaw puller, or you have to take up shoe polishing or go begging. If you are interested in these vocations, I have no objections." If they were not relenting, he used to cane them.

Some time later, the eldest son was adopted by a gentleman and since then he lived with his adopted father. After ten years, the adopted son (the eldest one) became an Engineer and the other two sons who lived with their natural father were still illiterates and became counter productive. Who is responsible for this muddle? It is essentially the natural father of course.

If the same father without taking recourse to negative suggestions, offered positive suggestions, they would have become engineers, doctors and collectors and if encouraged by father with an offer of some incentive to study properly, the results might have been different i.e. productive and encouraging.

So, hypnotherapy has a very great part to play with persons of this type i.e. nervous, apprehensive or hypersensitive and this has been proved beyond all reasonable doubt.

The inherent sickness is more often attributed to this kind of traumatic period.

The events or situations prevailing at the time of the birth of the boy or girl or during their childhood days:

During the early period of childhood the children usually crave for love, care, affection and protection from their parents. Some children even expect that their parents will never reject their just requests for their progress, and they would extend them all the necessary protection they need till they enter the adulthood. Meanwhile if anything goes wrong their grief know no bounds and they get mentally upset. The presence of another offspring in the house puts the child on tender-hooks and the doting affection of its parents towards the second child makes him an uneasy-sibling-rivalry. Any outburst from his side may be rejected by its parents. During these occasions he has to spend the days in the house uneasily, trembling and wavering mentally.

In another case, a father, a teacher by profession, used to offer less marks to his brilliant son for being his student, for fear of criticism. The son who was upset by the wrong done by his father in alloting marks, was unable to bear the brunt, and he became vindictive towards his friends.

Such revenge-prone children can be cured by hypnotherapy for their well being and progress.

The circumstances prevalent in the neighbourhood of a village, town or a city:

Every person plans to reach his cherished goal at some particular point of time during his life. If by any unexpected turn of events or obstacles or peculiar circumstances which may prevail at that point of time and he could not achieve his desired goal, he will be subjected to strange and unusual mental conflict, trauma, and becomes dull, desolate and dejected. A kind of "inferiority complex" will set in him and he underestimates his capacities and faculties, and suffers by comparison. He becomes fickle minded, his behaviour changes every now and then causing not only discomfort to himself but great concern to people around him.

Too much exhaustion and worry keeps him irritant and dull. He loses interest in everything and mentally gets crippled.

The mental sickness of a person or persons will be having a lot of reaction or commotion and cause disturbances in the society where the person or persons reside.

An example may illustrate the point in question. The eldest son belonging to an orthodox Hindu family was employed as an

41

engineer in a Public Sector Undertaking. A girl of a different community was his colleague and she used to maintain cordial relations with him. The events moved so fast that a decision was taken by them to get married soon with each other.

The boy was hesitant to inform his parents about his decision to marry a Muslim girl. He finally took courage to tell his mother the same, who conveyed the news to his father. The father became furious, reprimanded his son and advised him to change his mind. His mother and sisters in their turn pleaded to change his proposal to save the lives of their parents and thus maintain the dignity of the family. He sympathised for their feelings but clearly stated that if he is not going to marry that girl she will commit suicide. His father threatened that he would be run over by a train a day before the actual date of marriage of his son. Finally the engineer son and his girlfriend got married to each other in the Registrar's office, without the consent of the parents.

Unfortunately from that moment onwards the members of both the families have disowned the newly married couple. The mental conflict and worry of the married couple was unbearable. The members of the society looked at them as if they were murderers. The atmosphere in the office also was not of a welcome nature. Only two or three employees of the firm were friendly to the couple but others almost neglected them and treated them as nonexistent. As a result she resigned from her job and remained a housewife just to mitigate her mental worry and tension. The engineer had to lead a mechanical life, lacking the bonds of affection from his relatives, for his mental solace and satisfaction.

After the marriage of his son with the Muslim girl, the health of the aged father deteriorated. The mother was also not well. Both of them had body pains, blood pressure and suffered from annoying dreams. Their family doctors advised them to maintain calm equilibrium and poise but of no avail. At last a hypnotherapist came to their rescue and brought succour to the aged parents by his treatment. There are still many families facing similar situations, and took to smoking and drinking assuming that their sufferings would be over but they are mistaken. They only get spoiled.

Those who are not superstitious or totalistic, those who can cope up with such serious situations and those who can put up with trifling affairs as they are aged and experienced, can maintain their physical and mental health with equanimity. But if they feel excited, crave for status and tight lipped over situations which are beyond their control, they have to face dismay and frustration in the end because of their bottled cautions.

In the West, doctors advise their patients to learn and practise "self-hypnotism" which is also known as "auto-suggestion". By means of self-hypnotism people can solve their own problems themselves and especially it is a boon for neurotic patients, according to Dr. Frank S. Lacron, the famous American hypnotherapist. More can be learnt about self hypnotism in the subsequent chapters.

Every human being has problems. The problems may be concerning with one's own family affairs, or financial situation or society. Some get scared and fretful over such problems and suffer with ailments, while some fortunate persons retain their cheerful moods without the aid of doctors. One has to strike a balance with the changing times and try to find a solution to the problem on hand. Problems and events by and large are same to the mankind. What makes the difference is how one reacts to them. Only then, one can safely come out of murky situations with the power of thinking and their introspection. An English poet has stated thus — "Life is a game. Play it with a smile". If this principle is observed in letter and spirit, there will be happiness all around. If one rejects this suggestion, diseases, fear, and phobias will come to the surface and necessitate the services of a hypnotherapist.

Mental Sickness

The great English poet Shakespeare beautifully divided the stages of a man into seven categories. The psychologists also divided the different stages of human behaviour and clarified succinctly. But the psychologists gave credence to the classification evolved by Elizabeth B. Herlock as the standard one.

1. Infancy — from the birth of a child to 3 weeks

2. Babyhood — the period upto 3 years

3. Early childhood — the period between 3 and 6 years

4. Late childhood — the period from 6 to 10 years

5. Puberty — the period from 10 to 13 years

6. Early adolescence — the period from 13 to 17 years

7. Late adolescence — the period from 17 to 21 years

8. Youth — the period from 21 to 40

9. Middle age — the period from 40 to 60 years

10. Old age — the period from 60 years till death

As far as mental diseases are concerned, it can be stated that the first three periods are considered to be safe. From the fourth period the human being understands things according to his views or perception.

The negative or unpleasant events that occur during the 4th and 5th period of age in one's life, will haunt the person through out his life. The events or situations experienced during this period will create a firm impact on his mind and that in turn may result in weakening the individual in life. The well known psychologists like Freud and Young emphasized this point of view quite authoritatively.

Those who belong to the age group of 5 and 6 will be having the relevant physical and mental changes, acquiring an acceptable individuality of their own. At this age, the well disciplined parents and their character will mould the individual's behaviour which in turn shape their future to a great extent. If the parents are not so disciplined, or if they have committed any anti-social act, anti-social behaviour or victims of bad habits or addiction to vices, their children inherit 90% of such addiction-to-vices. The shadows of elders, good or bad, will obviously fall on the lives of their children. This view is supported by eminent scientists.

The prime duty of the hypnotist is to enquire how and when his patient has acquired a particular malady, then have a full grasp of the case history so that he can find the ways and means to be adopted to bring relief to the patient. If the hypnotist knows the case history, he can extend relief to the patient in the deep hypnotic trance by means of a technique called "Age Regression". In this method the hypnotist can obtain the necessary information from the patient. This helps in curing the disease by removing the unpleasant thoughts, fears which have been haunting the mind of the patient and by giving positive suggestions. The dramatic phenomenon of Age-regression has been adopted from times immemorial.

Stage hypnotism — Age regression process

Very recently I have treated one military officer in Chandigarh, aged 50 years, who normally speaks freely to the people, but feels nervous to talk to people with long and burly moustache. The very sight of such persons makes him mum and the silence pervades the whole atmosphere till such burly moustached person leaves the place. I have hypnotised him and applied "Age-regression" process. I gave step by step suitable suggestions, decreasing his age by one year every time, and asked him "Are you still afraid of the man having long and burly moustache?" The patient answered "Yes". Then I further reduced his age through suggestions in a phased manner and took him to the age of 12. He could successfully recall the incidents that had happened at the age of 12. Then I questioned "Are you still afraid of the man with long moustache? He said "No" to my surprise. At this particular point of time I had asked him some more questions and obtained the correct reason for the fear, from the patient. The patient declared that when he was aged twelve, his teacher having a big moustache canned him for no fault of his, in the presence of other students, and used to insult him profusely. He developed aversion for those people having moustache of the type his teacher had and refrained from their company or association altogether. Then I gave him suitable suggestions and cured the patient of his aversion towards such people with long moustache, once for all.

Hysterical Neurosis

It is a relic of the nineteenth century to consider hysteria a serious illness. It is one of the many possible symptoms of a neurosis and may appear in one of its many forms in highly anxious and emotional people. It is usually a physical symptom and one which diverts attention from an underlying mental conflict.

In 1895, when Breuer and Freud published their *Studies of Hysteria*, such an effect was explained as being "the result of repressed memories with the painful ideas converted into physical symptoms". All this suggests that hypnotherapy may provide the means for relief. This is correct, so long as the therapist remembers that the underlying neurosis must first be considered. Otherwise one could well get rid of the present hysterical symptom only to have the patient come back with another problem a few days later.

Some people are of the view that the hysterical patients can find relief and be cured of it when they are married. This is a misconceived notion because the hysterical conditions continued to appear even after marriage, in some cases.

A person who cannot solve some critical problems, suppress his desires in his daily life, due to lack of energy or stamina. He criticises himself and the people around him and in so doing acquires some illness. With the result, he develops worry and anxiety. Such people find some relief under the guise of such illness and manage to postpone the idea of solving of such problems. When they are examined by doctors, the doctors do not find any illness at all, these persons sometimes are prone to commit suicide.

As the physical and mental symptoms of hysteria are many, it is not possible to mention all. However among physical symptoms, tearing of clothes, grinding the teeth, crying, biting, laughing, distorting facial features, vibrating head, excessive anxiety, etc. are visible. Among mental symptoms of hysteria, emotional excitation, loss of complete memory, sexual distortions, etc. can be seen in the patient.

After detailed analysis the psychologists have noticed that emotional tension, feelings of defective discipline, maladjustment with family members or society, sexual dissatisfaction, frustration, are the main causes for hysteria.

An instance can clarify the point still further. There was a medical practitioner near my house. Unfortunately one day his wife caught fire. The doctor tried his level best to save his wife but in vain. From then onwards the doctor thought that he lost energy in his hands. If not he could have saved his wife from the flames. He imagined that his hands had been paralysed and hence he could not raise them. He was telling his doctor friends the same thing. But they vehemently disagreed with him. He discontinued his medical practice and confined himself to sick bed. Finally, I cured him of all his imaginary ailments.

The hypnotherapists in other countries have been curing such ailments stated above, and treating patients who have a marked predisposition to develop such ailments.

■ ■

Fears and Phobias 5

P hobia is a morbid fear or aversion. Phobia also means an irrational, abnormal, excessive and persistent fear of some particular object or situation.

Everyone is subject to fears at times, which could not be classified as "neurotic". These fears have logical and protective reasons. Anxiety or fear without some definite ground for it, is protective as are phobias, but they are also neurotic symptoms. If you inquire friends you will find that most of them have some phobia, major or minor.

We can overcome certain phobias, even if nothing is going to happen in a specific case, by adopting some preventive measures. For example, one may have a heart attack, but to reduce one's chance of having such an unpleasant experience it is important to keep one's weight down, exercise regularly, avoid cigarettes and eat a nutritious diet.

According to Edmund Jacobson, fears may become prolonged and excessive. Then they constitute a burden on the nervous system and may lead toward disorders in other systems as well. There comes a stage in certain cases where it becomes difficult to say whether the fear is merely an exaggerated normal state or a somewhat pathological one. But if the individual fears that he may jump out of a window when in high buildings or that he may stab somebody if a knife lies about, we can say that fear is definitely pathological and label it a phobia.

How does the method of relaxation apply to conditions of fear — normal or abnormal? The answer can be illustrated by the case history of an attorney who had amassed a small fortune, having lived a modern life of rush which involved protracted hours of attention to business. While still in his thirties, he complained that in so doing he had "burnt himself out" — had permanently impaired his vitality. Fatigue was frequently present, but most noticeable were fears, particularly when he was speaking at court or working in high buildings.

"Worry" is the complaint perhaps most often heard by the doctor in the field of nervous medicine. Can modern science contribute anything toward the solution of the problem of worry? In the past, most laymen and many doctors were inclined to believe that the only way to remedy worry was to "remove the cause" and that the cause of worry lay solely in the difficulties which we met, in life. But too often such provision is not feasible. Furthermore, certain losses cannot be remedied at all, for example, the death of a loved one. And in every life, trying situations inevitably arise from time to time. We are faced with the fact that practically the same kind of dangers and losses will lead one person to extreme worry and irritability but leave another relatively calm and self-possessed.

Granted, that worry is a subjective state which is incited but not wholly caused by various matters which arise in the lives of everyone, what can be done about it? In many, worrying becomes a habit; reassurance and argument commonly seem of little avail; the more they talk, the more, at least in some cases, does the worry seem to recur. Most of the persons tend to review the troublesome matter again and again, even if only the imaginative one, in an effort to find a solution. To escape such thoughts, they often resort to change of scene, to distracting occupation, to exercise and baths, per chance to drink or to sedative drugs; but mostly the problems of the worrisome individual are not solved.

If fortune favours or if time heals the wound, a new source of distress soon appears on the horizon—to be followed by one after another. The worrying tendency persists and even finds something new to feed upon.

Observation on worried patients suggests that their moments of concern involve in particular the knitting of the brows often, although this tension occurs commonly in most persons when they are thinking actively or facing a relatively bright light. It may be of interest to note how often this tension in this region is significant, noting that the animal which frowns or contracts his brows is meeting a difficulty. Under this assumption, if a worrisome patient reports or seems to show such tension more or less habitually, he is drilled particularly in relaxing this region.

We are sometimes told that the only way to find out why a person is melancholic or has certain fears, habits or worry or other emotional symptoms is to search his past for psychic causes. Such assumptions are not part of the approach described in this volume. Rather, our method is to observe what the patient is doing muscularly at the moment when his melancholy, fear, worry or other mental symptoms are present, and if we can identify particular patterns of contraction, however slight, we proceed as best as we can to eliminate them. If successful in this elimination, as edged by objective standards, we find that the symptoms tend to disappear.

If you are a worrier or are slightly inclined to "the blues", there probably are many issues which concern you needlessly, perhaps producing sleeplessness for many hours in the night. It may seem to you that you must find the answer to some problems in hand or that somehow you must overcome a certain source of irritation. Perhaps the issue is—"To be or not to be–That is the question!"

The best way that I know to handle morbid states of worry

is to keep in mind the distinction between the issue and the attitude. You must observe that at such moments your attitude is overtense. If you relax the excess tension present in various muscle groups, you attain a quietude of demeanour and you are likely to report a lessened interest in the issue. Questions that seemed fundamental, crying for an answer, may still appeal to your intellect but no longer affect your emotions so intensely. With habits of advancing relaxation, you tend to become able to adjust yourself to the living conditions you meet, perhaps not approving those conditions, but nevertheless not permitting them to render you overemotional and unfit. I find, however, that the learner needs to be reminded over and over again, when he becomes engrossed in a troublesome matter, to distinguish between the issue and the attitude.

Phobias

Phobic anxiety or phobia is an irrational fear. The patient knows it is unnecessary. Nevertheless he is unable to overcome this fear. It occurs without logic in situations which normally should not cause fear. Sometimes situations which merely resemble the original, or even thinking of such situation may cause similar fear. Phobias, in a person who is anxious or depressed, can often make him feel more anxious and more depressed. This is a very important factor in deciding treatment because if the underlying problem is one of depression, then it is certainly necessary to use anti-depressant drugs before attempting hypnotherapy.

Medical dictionaries list between 250 and 300 phobias but of course one can become phobic about anything given the right situation and emotional background. The above behavioral technique can be applied to the entire range of phobia illness and to any degree of fear from mild anxiety to utter panic. What is not generally recognised is the overwhelming anxiety and incapacitating physical effects that a phobia illness can cause.

The inhibitory principle can be applied in other situations where fear is present. Dr. Joseph Wolpe in his book *Psychotherapy by reciprocal inhibition* advocated an excellent method of working through fears and phobias and eliminating them.

Dr. Wolpe asks a patient to write out a list of everything which is frightening, disturbing or embarrassing him in any way. Omitting situations which would frighten anyone such as being attacked. The patient then is to rewrite the list in the decreasing order in terms of intensity.

In self therapy, this technique can be used to overcome fears and phobias. However, phobias are best handled by locating their causes, recalling the experience or experiences which generated them, and, discharging the accompanying emotions.

Phobias mainly develop from past experiences, sometimes from conflicts and possibly from suggestions to a child aimed at making it afraid of something. If a parent is phobic about some situation, the child may pick up from the present—partly from identification, and partly from suggestion. That is if the parent is afraid, then the situation is dangerous and the child should also be afraid. Always there is a confused wrong thinking in interpreting the situation, and it is regarded dangerous.

Fears may be quite normal, but sometimes they tend to be abnormal and in extreme and irrational cases, they become phobic. Dr. Wolpe's method of "desensitising" can be accomplished readily with self-treatment and is better applied to fears rather than phobias. You are quite likely to be the uncomfortable possessor of some phobias, for they are common. If you are claustrophobic and you cannot enter an elevator, you will do much stair climbing. This development is usually related to some childhood fright, usually mingled with other related experiences.

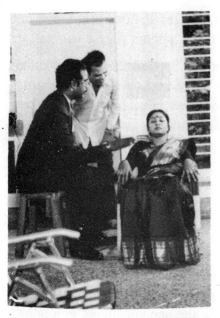
Hypnosis for phobias — Questioning Technique

Phobias are often easily overcome by employing the methods mentioned here. Identify the cause by your "Questioning technique". With self hypnosis regress yourself and go through the experience several times until you have worked off the emotions associated with it. Those who are afflicted with phobias are treated in our clinic by post hypnotic suggestions. I have treated several patients suffering from these phobias, and, now they don't even remember the phobia they had before.

Some Phobias and Their Names:

Air	Aero Phobia
Animals	Zoo Phobia
Being afraid	Phobo Phobia
Blood	Haemato Phobia
Books	Biblio Phobia
Cats	Ailuro Phobia
Darkness	Nycto Phobia
Death	Thanato Phobia
Dirt	Myso Phobia
Disease	Patho Phobia
Dogs	Cyno Phobia
Enclosed space	Claustro Phobia
Fire	Pyro Phobia

54

Flying	Aero Phobia
Food	Sito Phobia
God	Thoo Phobia
Heart disease	Cardio Phobia
Insanity	Mania Phobia
Lighting	Astrapo Phobia
Marriage	Gamno Phobia
Mind	Psycho Phobia
Nakedness	Gymno Phobia
Open space	Agora Phobia
Precipices	Maieusio Phobia
Rain	Ombro Phobia
Sexual intercourse	Ceito Phobia
Sharp objects	Belono Phobia
Skin diseases	Dermatosio Phobia
Sleep	Hypno Phobia
Snakes	Ophidio Phobia
Society	Anthro Phobia
Spirits	Demono Phobia
Stealing	Klepto Phobia
Surgical operations	Ergasio Phobia
Venereal intercourse	Venere Phobia
Young girls	Partheno Phobia
Water	Hydro Phobia

At present there are very many famous people suffering from phobias, but it would not be fair to name them. I would like to mention some famous phobics, whose names are recorded. Queen Elizabeth I had a rose phobia, while James-I became terrified at the sight of a sword. Eminent Psychoanalyst Sigmund Fraud had fear of travel and Pascal suffered from agoraphobia.

Crime Detection Through Hypnosis

Generally people enquire whether there is any possibility of obtaining secrets or vital material or information from a subject when he is in a somnambulistic condition. As a matter of fact, this is an important issue to deal with. But the subject never recalls such important information even though he is in a deep trance because it is harmful for him.

Let us suppose that the police are interrogating a person accused of murder, to elicit the truth. He never reveals the truth and never enters the stages of hypnosis, light, medium or a deep state. Even if the police threaten him, he never goes into trance. He only pretends. He only whispers a practical joke. Even if we put him into a deep trance he won't reveal anything that would endanger or harm his own interest.

Some time back one millionaire was murdered in Ahmedabad. The police immediately entered the scene and started investigating and interrogating the suspects. They finally concluded that the millionaire was murdered by his son-in-law. He was taken into custody, locked up in the police station and was beaten black and blue, tortured him in several ways, so as to get any clue from him. Finally, a senior police officer phoned to a known hypnotists of the place and asked whether he can try to get the truth from the son-in-law, the suspect, by the tenets of hypnosis. The so-called hypnotist who had not mastered even the rudiments of hypnotism guaranteed that the truth about the murder could be obtained by him and he professed to that extent.

As per the suggestions of the hypnotist, the suspect went into a supposedly deep trance and declared that the son of the deceased shot him four times. The dying father-in-law requested the son-in-law who was present on the scene to own the responsibility of the murder. The police officer recorded the whole statement on tape.

In fact the son-in-law's statement was incorrect. The son of the deceased had not shot his father with the said revolver. Moreover the son was not in the city on that fateful day. The fictitious version of the statement of the son-in-law was only an attempt to save his skin and to come out of the death trap and nothing else. If one can get the truth in such sensational session, everyone who has the necessary tenets of hypnotic technique can be employed in every police station of our country.

Is Hypnotism a Panacea?

So far we have discussed about mental ailments and its antecedents. We also bestowed some attention on how to cure the mental diseases by hypnotherapy. This gives rise to a doubt in the minds of enthusiastic people whether the hypnotherapy is useful for physical ailments also. Strictly speaking, diseases connected with atmospheric pollution, malnutrition and those of hereditary nature cannot be mitigated by hypnotherapy. For example diseases like T.B., malaria, cholera, leprosy, asthma, dermatitis (skin diseases) etc. can't be cured with the help of hypnotism because these diseases have no relation or connection with mental activity. No mental aberration can be connected to the incidence of these diseases. The different kinds of malnutrition, afflictions and other illnesses can be diagnosed and treated effectively by medical practitioners only and they do not come under the purview of the hypnotists. If any enthusiast comes forward claiming that he can cure them with hypnotherapy, then one can easily conclude that it is an exaggerated claim.

When I mentioned this point during the scientific hypnotic show organised by some of the patrons of the science, one hypnotist from the audience stood up and said that my statement was not true. He added that he had cured the headache of a woman who came to him to seek help through hypnotherapy. He taught her the technique of self-hypnotism which he claimed had cured her illness finally.

I did not react to his statement, reason being he was a local man and I was a stranger to that city. Even if I said anything to make the matter clear, the audience might not agree with me. The local hypnotist was speaking with conviction. So, I said to the audience "The statement has nothing to do with my performance here. I have come here not to cure the diseases but to give a scientific hypnotic show which you can see and enjoy. This show is only arranged for your enjoyment. I will meet the local hypnotist later on and explain him about hypnotism and other relevant matters." Then I continued the show on that day.

After the show that particular hypnotist came to me. He was neither an MBBS nor an RMP. He was not even a diploma holder in psychology. I was discussing with him the difference between physical and mental ailments. Meanwhile a gentleman rushed to us and told him that his wife was seriously ill, he should immediately visit the patient. The patient was the same person whom the local hypnotist was supposed to have cured of her headache. The local hypnotist requested me to accompany him and treat his patient. But I declined. I advised him to consult a medical doctor. Or else, the woman patient would have to face serious consequences for lack of appropriate and timely medical aid. Time was an essential factor and so I sent them away promptly.

I was told that the woman patient in question was rushed to Nizam Orthopaedic Hospital, Hyderabad, and the doctors diagnosed her disease. She was suffering from a brain tumour. During the initial stages of that tumour, she used to have headache and took tablets to lessen the headache. But the headache continued. The family members thought that she was having some mental worry or trouble and so they took her to a local hypnotist (who met me in the hypnotic show). Without knowing the antecedents of her ailment or disease, he hypnotised her and taught her self-hypnotism to cure herself of the disease. The pain of course lessened a bit but the brain tumour which was already there worsened her condition.

Later, I came to know that the patient who was operated upon expired after a month. Had she approached the medical doctors earlier, she might have lived. This was due to the carelessness of the hypnotist, who had not understood the limitations of this science.

According to the rules of International Hypnotists Association, when a patient approaches a hypnotist for consultation, the hypnotist should enquire about the antecedents of the disease to make sure that the patient is not suffering from any physical ailment and after confirmation of that by clear analysis, should he start the treatment with the aid of hypnosis.

The hypnotist should first look at the case history of the patient, ascertain the disease from its symptoms, find out whether that disease is physical or mental. An experienced hypnotist can understand all this. If the hypnotist gets any perceivable doubt regarding the condition of the ailment or nature of the disease, he should refer it to a competent medical doctor for clarification.

In the same way, a patient should first approach a doctor to find out whether his or her ailment is physical or not, and then only approach a right hypnotist for relief. Fortunately, there are few eminent hypnotherapists in our country and hence there is no possibility of any unfortunate event to happen in our country like the one cited above. At the same time, the people should be aware of the presence of pseudo-hypnotists who boast of bringing total relief from ills of both psycho and soma.

■ ■

Hypnotism and Occult 6

Generally people believe that by learning hypnotism, one can acquire spiritual powers and by using the same, can recall the details of one's previous birth. Some hypnotists with no clear understanding of hypnotism proudly declare that they have hypnotised their subjects to know the events which occurred in their previous births. Such uttering of platitudes are of no use. It is only a misconception and nothing else. Some novelists and film makers propagate this idea to suit the whims and fancies of their tribe.

One well known author had published a novel some twenty five years ago, wherein he hypnotises the heroine and obtains details of her eighteen previous births. The readers were led to believe this misconceived stuff which created waves of doubt and fear in the minds of the readers belonging to Europe. As a matter of fact the said novel was a piece of fiction.

A novelist of London, who was also a stage artist, learnt hypnotism, propagated the theme of knowing one's previous birth by hypnotism, and, conducted shows in every town. During the course of the show he used to hypnotise a girl and ask her what was her mother tongue. She declared it was English. Then he hypnotised her and send her into deep trance and asked what was her mother tongue in her previous birth. She answered it was French. The innocent audience believed the show with mirth and frolic and used to clap their hands with much gusto. The girl used to answer only in English. The said stage artist engaged the same girl for conducting all his shows. This gave rise to suspicion among some alert members of the audience and later they came to know that the girl was the assistant of the said stage hypnotist. The stage hypnotist was given a good bashing.

But one can hypnotise a person by taking recourse to age regression method, the period year by year. By extending suitable suggestions one can obtain some of the events or facts that occurred during the period of the childhood of the concerned subject, and nothing more than that.

There are now physical research laboratories in almost all developed countries of the world. Also, there were indications that Russians were contemplating to send messages through telepathy to the cosmonauts in space ships and thus trying to reduce much expenditure. Laying it aside and before taking up the issue of whether there are supernatural powers or any semblance of its existence in this world, let us now discuss whether we can achieve them through hypnotism. According to hypnotists, a person can be hypnotised and made to attain the deep hypnotic state so as to bring out the amazing hidden powers in him.

In the past, people used to believe in supernatural powers. Also, mesmerists not only professed that they were having supernatural powers but with the blessings of God, they could transmit such powers to the selected persons. The innocent folk flocked to them with affirmation.

The mesmerists were maintaining a list of supernatural powers, similar to the menu cards of restaurants. Some of the items mentioned in the lists were as follows.

Telepathy

It is a coincidence between two persons' thoughts, a transmission of thought independently on the recognised channels of sense. This conception spread so widely that many people conceive it now as something distinct from thought transference and claim a line of division with the following argument; in telepathy the transmitter is often unaware that he acts as an agent and the receiver does not consciously prepare himself for the reception. Telepathy cannot be made a subject of experiments while thought transference can.

Clairvoyance

It is a supernormal mode of perception which results in a visual image being presented to the conscious mind. The perception may be of objects or scenes or forms distant in space or in time, past or future. There will be coincidental truth in the visual perception and (in some cases as in dreams or principally in trance) consciousness is absent and forms may not only be distant in space or time but be altogether on another plane of existence.

Precognition

It is the ability to sense future events psychically. Scenes forming the future may unfurl in dreams or visions, a prediction may be given by a disembodied voice, or a person may have a sudden hunch that something is going to happen. Sometimes there are undefined feelings of mental or physical stress before a disaster.

Premonition

The unpleasant side of precognition. It is the ability to sense unpleasant events like deaths, assassinations, catastrophes etc. Two hundred people in England had premonitions, most of them coming in dreams, of the 1966 coal slide that killed 144 adults and children in Aberfan, Wales. Abraham Lincoln also could predict his death.

Psychokinesis

Mind over matter. Also known as PK, it is the ability, by purely psychic means, to change the composition of physical objects, animate or inanimate, or move them around in space. Two examples of PK are "willing" specific numbers to come up when dice are thrown and impressing mental images on unexposed film. It has also been theorized that the human mind (and possibly to animal mind) can psychokinetically influence future events, but there is no conclusive proof of this power.

Auto-writing

It is the most tremendous exhibition of "unconscious muscular action". Scripts are produced without the control of the conscious self. It is one of the highest and most valuable spiritual gift, if reliable, it opens up a direct channel for obtaining teachings from the "Beyond". Between these two extremes many problems of a complex nature present themselves to physical research.

Prevision

Foreknowledge of the future acquired in a visual form. Such visions are mostly spontaneous. But there are means of experimentally inducing them through crystal gazing and other forms of divination.

Astral body

According to a widely held theory among those who study psychic phenomena, every person has a duplicate body within his physical organism, exactly like the physical body in every way but made of finer and lesser dense material. Also called the "etheric" or "second" body or "the double", the astral body has much greater freedom of movement than the parent body.

As a matter of fact, the different powers or items mentioned above and their explanations are true. But if a person aspires to get these powers by means of hypnotism, it will be equivalent to imprudence, ignorance and a blunder.

In the sphere of hypnotism there is no scope to achieve or conquer the supernatural powers. If any one has exhibited such supernatural powers with the help of hypnotism, it might be an accidental one. Hypnotism is a science and considered very near to medical literature.

But one thing is real, the use of hypnotherapy can bring a marvellous change in a human being. A person with had habits earlier, may now turn to be a pious person after proper hypnotherapy. His thinking faculties may improve. He may be able to solve some intricate problems or issues with greater ease. If any one feels otherwise it will be a myth/fallacy.

After the advent of Dr. Braid the influence of pseudo hypnotists or fake hypnotists had dwindled but a semblance of the said belief had its roots in the minds of the general public.

Subconscious Mind

What is man's place in this utterly mysterious and ever expanding universe? The statement coming from the mind of an eminent scientist, Dr. Robert A. Millikan, has evidential value— "We have come from some where and we are going some where. The great Architect of the universe never built a stairway that leads to nowhere". Dr. Edward Signoth of Yale from another discipline of science, that of biology, supports the assumption that "Purpose is inherent in the life process." "All our dignity exists in thought", said Pascal. "On earth there is nothing great but man, in man there is nothing great but mind", writes Sir William Hamilton.

The enquiring mind in itself is a wonder. Is it reasonable to assume the absence of a planner when the plan is evident? Did infinite mind preside at the birth of the Universe? Why violate the basic assumption of the human mind? *Ex nihile nihil fit* (from nothing, nothing comes).

Mind has its roots in and emerges from a field of reality which transcends space, time, and, continuum. Mind is the measuring rod of reality and is limited in its action and expression only by the nature of its own being. While this insight has an obscure place in our present day intellectual climate, it is not new. It is found at the centre of every great religious tradition. It is the great intuition grounded deep in the structure of personality. It follows because of its inherent nature. The human mind has more potential than we ordinarily believe and that it has powers seldom recognised, and it functions in a border-land area, greater in extent and significance than that revealed by our day to day awareness.

Mind is the measuring rod of reality. In fact, mind is the only reality in a world of changing matter. The force behind all progress and achievement is energy applied by mind. If correctly used, your mind will bring you whatever you want or need.

Thinking, a mental activity is not the result of processes originated in the brain. Memories are not stored in the brain. In fact, there is no anatomical evidence that man has a mind. The realms of mind are not confined to man's skull. Thinking is not done by brain, it is accomplished by mind or consciousness. Mind is certainly not identical with brain, it belongs to a totally different category of reality.

Consciousness is the ultimate unit of which all matter is spun. We must therefore assume that consciousness is a thing in itself. Regardless of where you look, you are looking with your mind. Matter as such is not what you see but the way in which you are seeing reality. Consciousness is the ultimate substance of the universe. It operates without our body as the focal point.

The basic question is, can mind illuminate its own path, select the direction in which it will go, or is man a helpless puppet in the hands of his own body? It is to mind or consciousness that we must look for the key, to know the meaning of life. As Milton said "The mind has its own place and in itself can make a Heaven of hell—a hell of Heaven". There is a passage in the *Bhagwad Gita (The Song Celestial)* which reads—*"Man is made by his beliefs - as he believes, so he is."*

The mainland is your conscious mind, the island is your subconscious one. It is on that island that you will experience peacefulness and relaxation. Will power is a function of the conscious mind.

The Freudian model of the mind includes three components, the Ego, the Superego and the Id. The Id says "Do it now", the Ego says "not now. This is not the appropriate time and place to do it", and the Superego says "Don't do it at all ever, it is evil and wrong to do it under any circumstances".

It was Pierre who originated the term "Subconscious", a claim Freud did not dispute. Pierre Janet worked in Paris where he used the term "Subconscious" in elaborating his theories of Psychopathology based on his extensive work with hypnosis.

The subconscious of which today's hypnotists speak, is the repository of forgotten memories, the source of the psyche's energy, the health-maintaining-serve-mechanism, and the programmable-bio-computer by which man can understand the mind, head it and direct it into its highest accomplishments.

The subconscious is not inventive, it works with automatic and unquestioning accuracy upon the plans and concept which are fed into it. It is completely unselfconscious, it does not know what it is, or even that it works. It only knows how to do, what it does, it never knows or cares why. It does not search for truth, it accepts all input data as though true. It cannot predict anything because it does not know anything outside its own experience. The subconscious mind does many things which conscious mind cannot do, and indeed the sum of all the conscious mind in the world cannot do. It is infinitely complex and beyond the full compression of the conscious mind. All that can be done is to learn to utilize its great powers intelligently.

It thus follows that the subconscious mind acts on what it believes or perceives to be true, and this belief could be based on a declarative statement than on inductive or critical reasoning.

Hypnotherapy is merely the wise and ethical application of certain mental principles which daily affect every human being. The facts and forces used in hypnosis are those which affect us also through tradition, ritual, society, advertising, education and all of the words, gestures and actions that comprise and form our total life situation. Hypnotism provides a rational way to eradicate the irrationalities of our lives:

* It provides a way to control purposefully for our wellbeing the very force of suggestion, which also can and some times does accidentally damage us.

* The harmful effects of suggestion on a mind made susceptible in any of the ways mentioned above, can be reversed through hypnosis. The power of suggestion is inadvertently and irrationally utilised by life in ways that often harm us.

* Hypnosis is a scientific way to use the same powers of suggestion to help us, for what improper-suggestions have caused, the proper-suggestions can correct.

How the Subconscious Thinks

If we expect to influence the subconscious with the aim of self benefit it is important to understand the way it works. At times, it seems to be somewhat childish and immature. It takes everything entirely literally.

When a person is in hypnosis, the subconscious seems to be near the surface, or sometimes may largely have taken over conscious thinking, as it does writing in automatic writing. If a person in the waking state is asked the question, "Would you tell me where you were born?" He will almost invariably answer by naming the place. He interprets the question as a desire to know the location and names it. In a fairly deep state of hypnosis, the person would reply by saying "yes" or more likely would merely nod. That is the correct literal answer "yes" he is willing to tell you. It is a good example of how the subconscious takes things literally.

Psychiatrists have insisted that the first six years of life are crucial in forming the personality, and that by age six, many psychological and personality factors are unalterably established.

As we grow up, learn and nurture, our conscious view points about many things which undergo change. The subconscious may also change its view, but more often will retain those of childhood. If something happened to you at the age of six, your subconscious is likely to continue to look at it with the view-point of a six years old.

A childhood incident where one is frightened perhaps by a snake, may develop into a phobia about snakes which will persist causing the person to go into a panic at seeing a harmless grass snake. Consciously, the person recognises that some snakes are harmless, although repulsive. Even the picture of a snake could bring a panic reaction.

This brain, which is far more complex than any computer could ever be, has somewhere within it all the functions we call the subconscious mind. It can scan your past experiences, synthesize data in your memory bank, provide you with creative insights, and do a host of other incomprehensible things too, wonderful and numerous to mention even if we could. It is your success mechanism. Use it well.

A.R. Wallace records in his brief autobiography, *"I remember the very spot which I read in my carriage, when to my joy the whole solution came to me!"* About the same period Darwin appears with the achievement of discovering the theory of evolution and his first clear idea of this conception was in his bed, during an attack of malaria. James Watt who invented the principle of vapour power said the idea which made it possible to create a locomotive developed in his mind with compelling clarity as his mind was in a relaxed state during a quiet walk on a Sunday afternoon. Descart, the French mathematician and philosopher, is said to have made his great discoveries while lying in bed during morning hours.

The Creative Process and the Subconscious

It is now inferred in psychology that the conscious mind is just the emergent apex, the tip of an enormous and sustaining subconscious. Research has shown that the ability to bring into action this deeper area of the mind, determines the success of every worker, scientist, author, musician, inventor, or business magnet.

From the time of Socrates the founder of ethics, to the invention genius of Edison, Ford, Marconi, Einstein, this little understood and recognised area of mental activity has delivered the insight and know-how for almost every great achievement, which sustains modern civilization.

Charles Darwin, after years of investigation and observation, accumulated data which he believed pointed to a new and significant insight regarding the process of nature called "Evolution".

Thomas Edison who contributed so much to progress once said *"The key to successful methods come right out of, literally speaking, the air. A real innovation like an idea, a beautiful melody, is pursued out of space."*

The French Mathematician Henry Poincare described his creative work in almost the same terms. He stated that creative ideas did not come to him when he worked at his desk, but frequently flashed into his mind while he was engaged in other activities.

Dr. W.H. Rivers, the well known psychologist stated that many of the scientific ideas he valued most as well as the language in which they were expressed, came to him directly, in the half sleepy and half wakeful state continuous with definite sleep.

Before October 1920, medical science could offer no means of control or prevention of diabetes, the dreaded affliction of millions of people. During this period Frederick Grant Banting was teaching in the University of Toronto, in order to supplement the income from his meagre private practice. One night in October 1920 Young Banting was preparing his lecture for the following day. His subject was the then obscure affliction known as diabetes. His mind was a maze of conflicting theories, case histories and records of experiments with dogs. Working late, he went to bed and at two o'clock in the morning, he suddenly woke up, in his mind was a formula which when applied furnished a solution to his problem. This formula which he wrote in his note book immediately included three short sentences— *"Tie off the pancreatic duct of dog, wait six to eight weeks for degeneration, remove the residue and extract."* Turning off the light he immediately went back to sleep. It was this briefly stated formula which led to the discovery of insulin. Banting's conscious mind had come to grips with one of the baffling problems of medical science but could find no solution. His subconscious mind delivered to his conscious mind the method by which life and hope were extended to millions of afflicted persons. The significant fact is that following full consideration of all available

70

data, and while his conscious mind relaxed in sleep, his subconscious mind solved the problems.

After his dinner, Pasteur used to pace the hall and corridor of his room at the Ecole Normale, meditating on the details of his work. New insights or discoveries were frequently made when he was engaged in work not related to the immediate problems.

It is known that many important insights and concepts have arrived apparently by chance. Among such instances may be mentioned Fleming's understanding of the significance of penicillin.

Intuitions sometimes occur during sleep and a remarkable example is quoted by Cannon Otto Leewi. "One night with a brilliant idea, he reached out for a pencil and paper and jotted down a few points. The next morning he was aware of having an inspiration during the night, but to his consternation could not decipher his notes. All day at the Laboratory in the presence of familiar apparatus he tried to remember the idea and to understand the notes but failed. But during the night, to his great joy he again woke up with the same flash or insight. This time he carefully recorded it before going to sleep again.

The nearest, simplest, and most definite experiments in the history of biology brought proof of the chemical mediation of nerve impulses. This was the beginning of a host of investigations in many countries throughout the world on chemical intermediation, not only between nerves and the muscles and glands they affect, but also between nerve elements themselves.

The Creative Process in Music

Mozart confessed to a friend *"When I am, completely to myself, entirely alone, and of good cheer, it is out of one such occasions that my ideas flow best and most abundantly. Whence and how they come I know not, nor can I force them"*. Regarding

71

his inspiration, Mozart said *"Now I do hear in my imagination, the parts in sequence, but I hear them, as it were, all at once...what a delight that is, I cannot tell"*.

Rizard Wagner recorded that ideas for his musical competitions came to him "like a flash of light in the greatest clarity and definiteness, but not altogether in complete detail." In a letter to Fran Wesendonk he referred to the blissful dream state into which he fell while composing.

Beethoven clearly stressed the inadequacy of the rational mind for creativity. *"The new and original is born of itself without one's thinking of it"*. For W.T. Chopia, creation was spontaneous, miraculous, he wrote without foreseeing. It would be complete, sudden and sublime.

Tehaikorsky wrote *"Generally speaking, the germ of a future composition comes suddenly and unexpectedly"*. Many of his themes were invented and his works planned during long solitary walks. It was the emerging of subconscious insights and creativity that the renowned French Composer, Saint Saens was describing when he maintained that he had only to listen.

The treasure of all memories and experiences is in the subconscious mind. When it is highly sensitive and supernormally developed, we have a prodigy or genius, a Mozart or a Goethe. Often the creations of musicians, painters, writers and inventors are wholly the result of operations of the subconscious.

Dreams and Relevancy

The students of hypnotism should know about dreams and their relevance. A dream is a sequence of sensations, images, thoughts, etc. passing through a sleeping mind, a fanciful vision of the conscious mind, day dream, fantasy, a fond hope or aspiration, anything so lovely, charming, and transitory.

Usually dreaming is an activity of right half of the brain. It has been known for a long time that dreams can supply information about the conscious mind. We all dream, but some people are better at remembering them than others. To remember a dream means that the content of dream must pass from the right brain to the left brain. Again, the reason why dreams are difficult to remember probably has something to do with the function of the "corpus callosum."

When you dream, things are "real" as far as your emotions and reactions are concerned. Because you dream while you are asleep, your body is restricted in the responses it can make. It is usually restricted to heart beat, perspiration and breathing (those things controlled by autonomous nervous system). Even the bizarre, symbolic dream, often with impossible things happening together, appear to have its own internal logic, and the dream appears to be consistent within its own frame work.

The dreams do not use the reality of the left brain, nor do they use the logic and reasoning of the left brain. Dreams are a feature of the right brain and use largely symbols, emotions and synthesis as a mode of expression. Different things occur in the same scene because they unite to convey an impression–or even a message. The point I wish to stress is that, in so far as hypnosis is concerned, the right brain suspends the reality, then what is created in the right brain at that moment of time, becomes the reality.

The ideas which have been suppressed in the unconscious state and the experiences which have been obtained in the conscious state of a person can be re-animated in his dream. If that person is in a deep hypnotic trance, the hypnotist suggests relevant questions or gives suggestions as the case may be and the person tells aloud the experiences and ideas which are hidden or buried deep in his unconscious mind. That is the only difference which we have to notice in this connection.

Is there any relevance for one's dream? From times immemorial this question has haunted the minds of intelligentsia, scholars, scientists, reputed writers and they have expressed different opinions and views. From the Epic age onwards various views have been expressed. The effects of the dreams were causing terror to some people, brought luck and good-will to the others. Some people became very slow, dull and sluggish brooding over their dreams. Such belief was in vogue till the end of the nineteenth century.

During the early period of the 20th century, Freud made research over dreams and published a book. "*Interpretations of Dreams*". But Freud, exploring the problems later in greater depth, recalled that whilst in hypnosis, one of his patients had been able to retrace the origin of her father whom she had been nursing and to whom she was particularly attached.

The idea of dream interpretation had subsequently discarded the use of hypnosis entirely, to pursue the method known as free association. Nevertheless he maintained that if psychotherapy was ever to become widely available to the public, the use of hypnosis as a short-cut procedure would be essential.

In 1953, two Americans, Engene Aserinsky and Nathaniel Kleitman observed sleeping infants and noticed rapid and regular movement of the eye balls (R.E.M. Sleep) beneath the closed eyelids. They noticed the same phenomenon in adults, during electroencephalograph (EEG) recordings of these stages. They demonstrated some very special activity of the brain with very fast beta waves, upto twenty cycles per second.

This phase of sleep was called Rapid Eye Movement (REM) sleep and would last from ten to fifty minutes. We know that many important changes take place in the body during these stages. Aserinsky and Kleitman, curious to know what was going on, awakened those subjects at his point, who reported that they were dreaming. Moreover, they were able to give vivid

74

descriptions of the content of these dreams. These eye movements were similar to those of a person who is awake and looking around. It has therefore been suggested that in the REM phase it is as if the sleeper is viewing a play on the stage in his world of dreams.

Dream Interpretation

Another area which presented itself for investigation by Freud's ever curious mind was that of dream interpretation. Freud called out dreams *"The Royal road to the unconscious"*. He correctly observed that these dreams can lead us straight to the emotions buried deep in the unconscious. As his research continued, he came to recognise symbolic meanings of objects and activities in dreams and so was able to use them for diagnostic purposes.

Essentially, Freud claimed that dreams fulfil our deepest wishes in a way and may have a sexual meaning. He proposed an entirely new language of symbols for example, a house represents the human body. Trees, poles, weapons, motor cars and aeroplanes are masculine symbols and rooms, doors and caves represent female parts. Perhaps the most familiar example referred in the Bible is Joseph's interpretation of Pharaoh's dreams of seven lean cows and seven fat cows, and seven lean and seven fat ears of corn.

The obvious interpretation of the dream must be ignored according to Freud. Although we really know the meaning of our dreams, we fail to recognise that fact. We don't know that we know. So we think we don't know. What we experience, what we do, what others do, and what we see in dreams, are but symbols.

Moreover, although Freud developed his methods of dream-interpretation and of free association without the use of hypnosis, both these procedures may be utilised for considerable advantage in some hypno-analytic methods practised today. As indicated earlier, hypnosis provides a direct line of communication with the unconscious. Therapy is greatly speeded up and numerous other advantages have emerged which will be discussed later.

To discuss the points or events which occur in a person's dream, one has to ascertain the surroundings where he was born, his financial position, his association with males and females etc. Sometimes his desires which are hidden in his unconscious mind comes out in the form of dreams and offers him relief and satisfaction. A person who is optimistic may imagine numerous events which may occur in future and sometimes those may find place in dreams in advance. When one is awake he can clearly and vividly recall one's dreams.

A smoker may dream that he has given up smoking and his friends and family members congratulating him for not smoking. This dream indicates that he is having a strong desire not to smoke. He might have read the sentence "smoking is injurious to health" several times and the same might have remained in his unconscious mind. His unconscious mind is trying to see him give up his smoking habit but to no purpose. But the same desire appears in his dreams again and again and is giving him some satisfaction. A hypnotist can suggest him in a hypnotic trance and explain him in the form of suggestions the dangers of smoking and can gradually create an aversion towards smoking in his mind.

Some 600 people who have been trained by me at Balanandam Institute of Hypnotism are fully proficient in creating that kind of aversion towards smoking even among hard core smokers.

Dreams

A dream is a train of thoughts and fancies occurring during sleep, a vision something only imaginary, a reverie. Reverie is day-dreaming, fit of musing dreamy thinking or imagination especially of agreeable things.

An eminent psychologist, Dr. Aserinsky stated that during sleep a person can lessen physical exhaustion, mental tensions and stresses and get relief to a possible extent. Every person needs sleep because it gives a kind of soothing effect to strained nerves and keeps him or her in good shape both mentally and physically.

The Electroencephalograph (EEG) records one's feelings and experiences and other changes occurring during one's sleep.

An American psychologist — a well known hypnotist, Dr. William Kleiborn made EEG recordings and found out that there was no noticeable difference in the mental state of a person who was fast asleep and who was in a hypnotic trance. During sleep a person will be having his or her own ideas being reflected in sleep. But a deeply hypnotised person will carry out all the suggestions made by the hypnotist. Hypnotic state and sleep are distinct situations and while the subject is in the hypnotic trance he can also be further suggested into falling asleep, and his ideas or views will be in confirmation with the suggestions given by the hypnotist at that particular point of time.

When we go to sleep, throughout the night we will be dreaming. We can recollect some of those dreams and may forget the others completely.

According to Dr. William Kleiborn, those dreams that occur during the early morning hours can be remembered by all and these are important and relevant also. Our ancestors give credence to this aspect.

Dr. William further states his theory thus: we sometimes propose to attend a meeting or go out to meet a close friend. After leaving the house, on our way we will be observing numerous scenes. We will be having a chat with one or two of our close associates, do shopping on the way, visit a hotel to satisfy our appetite and finally attend the meeting. If any one enquired us as to what we had done during the previous day, we simply mention that we have attended a meeting.

Similarly many events take place in our dreams. As stated earlier we may meet some persons, talk to some others. We do not know them nor their destinations, but we reach our destination as per the terms of the dream. If we dissect and analyze the said dream we can come to an accurate conclusion as to the state of one's mind.

According to Freud, if a man observes bottles, pits, caves, mangoes, in a dream these symbols indicate that he is craving for the association of a woman. Similarly, if women in their dreams observe long poles, snakes, keys, swords and sweet items, these connote that they are aspiring for the association or company of the man of their choice. Some psychologists agreed with the views of Freud and some others rejected them altogether. But many hold the view that there is some relevance in the appearance of objects during the course of dreams and their symbolic meanings.

We may write any number of pages about dreams. But I have mentioned only some aspects concerning the dreams to the extent applicable to Scientific Hypnotism. We have to observe one important aspect here. Our ancestors preached that seeing fruits or flowers in a dream brings in luck, or one will be married if one sees a corpse in a dream. While these are opinions based on some personal experiences or traditions, one cannot certainly go by these freak experiences, as psychology of dreams as a science may have far more complex logic and explanation.

Some Buddhists have utilised the dream state to indicate the status of the human condition, vis-a-vis the nature of the ultimate metaphysical reality. And postulation and negative perception can prove to be more relevant for an analysis of the distinction among the real and dream objects.

Sigmund Freud

In Vedic literature the word *"Swapna"* (dream) was mentioned in the *Samhitas*, *Brahmanas* and the *Aranyakas*. The word *"Swapna"* conveys four distinct meaning from the context of its use, sleep, deep sleep, dream and deity. In Vedic literature there is deification of dreams and also attribution of symbolic reference to the external world.

This ancient Indian tradition quite plausibly anticipates the Freudian model, especially this concepts of content and dream formation.

■ ■

Memory & Concentration

$\mathcal{S}$ ome students ask me whether hypnotism can help improve one's memory power. I reply in the affirmative that memory power can be improved certainly by means of hypnotism. The present day youth is facing many problems like forgetfulness, and fear of examinations. Sometimes the young people proceed to study with negative suggestions in their mind. They feel that their memory is decreasing. They are afraid of it and so they invite forgetfulness. These types of learning problems can be reduced or eliminated with the help of hypnotherapy.

The major factors, low self esteem and lack of motivation are both covered extensively. Additional factors are, poor study habits, negative thoughts, absence of reward, medicine and drugs, and fear.

It is recognised by outstanding medical authorities that not less than 75% of causes of ill health are mental and emotional. It is a matter of common observation that a person's mental and emotional life is affected by the condition of his body and the environment in which he lives.

Memory is concerned with the recall of information that exists in the mind. Self-hypnosis can be useful both in learning and in recalling.

Hypnotherapy is merely the wise and ethical application of certain mental principles which affect every human being daily. It provides a rational way to eradicate the irrationalities in our

HARRY LORAYNE

Harry Lorayne — the memory wizard

personality. It provides a way to control purposefully for our well being, the very force of suggestion which also can and some times does damage us. The harmful effects of negative suggestions on a mind, made susceptible in any of the ways mentioned, can be reversed through hypnosis. The power of suggestion is inadvertently and irrationally misused in life for unfair purposes. Hypnosis is a scientific way to harness the same power of suggestions to serve us. Whatever damage that improper (negative) suggestions have caused, can be corrected by proper suggestions.

One cannot study and remember in a disturbed atmosphere or surroundings. An appropriate location for study and proper time frame to accomplish the task, are essential elements. One must have enough self confidence to become success-oriented. All these problems of learning can be reduced or eliminated through hypnotherapy.

Memory is concerned with the recall of information that exists in the mind. Learning is an operation of both right and left brains, though in the past it was strongly believed that it was an operation of the left brain only. Recall means to bring the information back into conscious awareness, i.e. allow the information back into the left brain. To facilitate recall, we need to create a situation which allows information to flow more readily from the right brain into the left. Self-hypnosis can be useful both in learning and recalling.

Let us first understand "recall". The memory functions best when it is relaxed. You will find that those things you wish to recall come more readily into your consciousness. This has probably something to do with the corpus callosum and the fact that, under hypnosis, you get the practice of passing information between the two halves of the brain and practice always makes this easy.

If there is something particularly important for you to remember, then put yourself into a hypnotic state and begin to think about the topic but do not consciously try to remember simply.

A simple illustration will be effective to make the point clear. Suppose you wish to remember a telephone number and for some reason, you have no access to the operator, or you do not know the address. This is a fairly common occurrence in day-to-day life. What you could do is hypnotise yourself and imagine a situation where you are ringing up the person. Begin with your decision to do so, as if going to the phone and dialling the number. In all likelihood the number will pop up in your conscious awareness. If you have the number in a book see yourself turning the page. The students who are to appear for the examination are sent into a deep trance like state to convince them that they will remember with unfailing accuracy all the subjects they have studied earlier, and infuse in them courage and self confidence. Such attempts by hypnotists will obviously yield best results, if adhered to correctly.

Accordingly, I hypnotised some ten indolent students of a high school in Hyderabad and offered positive suggestions to them so as to infuse in them self confidence. I obtained best results in this regard. Within a month seven students out of these ten turned out to be the best students in their classes and obtained first classes. The others failed to reach this level because of their continued indolent attitude towards studies and the disharmonious atmosphere prevailing in their families at that time.

The teachers as well as the parents have to offer such positive suggestions to their children to encourage them, motivate them to improve their mental faculties, and memory. They can see for themselves achieving some encouraging results. A ward's progress is in the hands of its teachers and parents.

How Memory Works

The subconscious mind is also the storehouse of memory. We record every perception when received, much like a motion picture with sound effects and even with all the other senses viz., sight, sound, touch, smell and taste. Under hypnosis the picture can be replayed.

When does memory begin? It is a pertinent question. Is it at a few months of age, a year or two, or can there be even earlier memories? Some physicians familiar with hypnosis are convinced that there is in the subconscious an actual memory of being born. Some even believe that there can be prenatal memories. Dr. Nandor Fodor tried to prove the existence of birth and prenatal memories through the interpretation and analysis of dreams.

In hypnosis, memories of forgotten past experiences can be recalled. The subconscious may punish you at times for things you have done, yet one of its duties is to protect you from harm. Memory makes many things.

Amnesia

Amnesia means loss of memory, forgetfulness, partial or total loss of memory caused by brain injury, or by shock, repression or any other trauma.

"Fight" against amnesia is within ourselves. Whatever one is — a man or woman, whether it is a child or grown up person, one can fight against amnesia. It is the human brain and his or her mental faculties will be there in good stead. This is a fact.

The only requisite is one has to apply a possitive suggestion instead of a negative one.

Only in some cases loss of memory occurs. It occurs to those whose brains have been injured in accidents, the aged, and to those who are addicted to alcohol and drugs. The loss of memory never occurs to healthy people including those who are attaining the age of maturity. If any one feels that he or she is bereft of memory then it means that he or she is nurturing a phobia to that effect. Such persons will be forgetting some events completely but recollect some other events correctly and with firm attention.

A student who forgets his science lessons, repeats successfully how many runs Sunil Gavaskar had made in a particular test match. A person who forgets that he owes a sum of sixty rupees to his friend, obviously remembers a small amount due to him from another person. A boy who forgets the items which his mother asked him to purchase from the provision stores, remembers every word stated to him by his girl friend. An elderly person who decries that he is unable to remember anything, accomplishes his daily chores in a systematic manner. If these are amnesic persons, they have to forget each and everything. But it is not so. It is only a kind of phobia. This problem can be corrected by giving themselves self suggestions.

Should one remember each and every thing? One need not have to remember every minute thing or event. It is sufficient if they can recollect most important things or events. You need not remember how much change is there in your money purse. You must remember how much money is there in your bank account. You need not remember how many steps are there in your staircase. But you should remember the way to your house. You need not remember how many Post boxes are there on the way between your office and house, but you should know in which Post box you have to post your letter.

According to Harry Lorayne, a memory expert, there are two kinds of memory (i) trained memory and (ii) untrained memory. If you clearly feel that you can remember a particular thing or event you can remember or recall the same at any time. If you are not willing to remember some thing or event, you will naturally forget them all.

You need not remember how many spokes are there in your cycle frame. Similarly, you need not remember how many buttons have been stitched to your shirt, you need not remember how many kilometers you are walking daily. Perhaps you may not be able to tell anyone in the affirmative. At the same time, you should not be perturbed and feel that you have amnesia. If a negative suggestion is infused in one's mind, he will be forgetting more things or events. Such things or events come under "untrained memory".

According to Harry Lorayne's theory to keep up one's memory is very easy. He conducted many Memory Workshops in U.S.A. and in Europe. He is still conducting the "Memory Workshops" with as much enthusiasm. He has introduced some "tips and tricks" and these are useful not only to students but also the employees.

First and foremost thing is, one has to feel that amnesia is a mere joke because we will not forget to take meals, counting currency notes, attending to daily chores. All these are necessary for one's sustenance and survival.

Generally loss of memory takes place in the field of one s research studies. In the first instance one reads more than what is actually required with fear complex.

Secondly one does not evince proper instance in his studies and so doesn't pay attention needed for studies. To attain memory one need not study a lesson ten times. It is unnecessary. If one studies three times it should normally be sufficient.

To illustrate this point, an example may suffice. In one school a group of students were standing in the playground and were conducting prayers. The Headmaster asked one student to count how many students were praying. After half an hour the student stated that 322 students were there. The Headmaster was overwhelmed with joy and asked the student how he was able to tell the number of students so correctly. The boy said promptly that he counted the legs of the students and divided it by two and arrived at the correct figure. This incident brings in some amusement. Here instead of counting the heads of the students, the boy counted the legs and divided the number by 2. In the same fashion the present generation of students without understanding a particular lesson, they read it ten times. Some students memorise the same. But it is enough to read a lesson three times to remember. During the first reading the student has to read it from beginning to end. During the second reading he or she should read the same with some understanding and concentration. Closing the book they have to review the same and recapitulate. During the third and final reading one has to apply a bit of more attention. Done this way, one cannot forget the lesson.

Due to tension and anxiety students forget in the examination hall whatever they have earlier read and retained in their memory. The students should get themselves a bit relaxed after receiving the question papers. Hypnotism will obviously cure such students who are vulnerable to fears and phobias. The encouragement given by the parents, making positive suggestions will certainly mitigate the fear in the students. Some times, the ardent belief in Gods and Goddesses will bring in more enthusiasm and cheer to the students and they do miracles in answering the papers.

Some memory tricks will help the students regarding the spelling of some words, like mathematics (mat-he-mat-ics). The link system or association of ideas, will be of much use to develop a sustaining memory.

Let us suppose that the mother of a boy might have asked him to bring tooth paste, soaps, mangoes and vegetables. Here the boy should remember the first letters of each item as T.S.M. and V. If the boy remembers the first letters of each item he can purchase the items from the market without putting the names of the items on paper. The boy can remember the items upto twenty if not more, by applying the link system of memory. The only thing is one has to train his mind and formulate a "code" or a link system or memory pegs. Such formulation of codes or link systems will bring happiness to the boy or girl as the case may be. It will improve their self confidence in leaps and bounds.

In foreign countries along with other systems of sports like Tennis, Cricket, Badminton, Chess, etc. the educational institutions have introduced memory games and encourage the students to take more interest in memory games by offering prizes and other incentives for their progress.

The role to be played by the parents to improve the memory of their children is greater than that of the teachers and lecturers. The parents' role is not a small one in producing and encouraging a cricketer like Sachin Tendulkar, an Indian chess prodigy like Vishwanathan Anand.

Once a Bank Officer of New Delhi paid a visit to me along with his wife and a ten year old boy. The mother began with a bang stating that her son was very poor at his studies and whatever he studied the previous day he forgot the next day. He would forget all that he had studied once he entered the examination hall. She further complained that if things continued in this manner he would end up as a failure in life. The father took the cue from his wife, got critical of his son. The boy looking down was shedding tears silently.

I tried to find out the truth from the boy himself. I asked the boy whether there was any truth in the statements of his parents about his studies and loss of memory. The boy replied thus "It is all true uncle, I could not retain whatever I study. The position is the same concerning all the subjects. I will be reading extensively with great care and after entering the examination hall every thing will evaporate into the thin air." I queried whether he is having any hobby to breed over. The boy replied with great enthusiasm "cricket Sir."

I was a bit elated. I asked him the place where the First World Cup cricket series were held. The boy said "In England in the year 1975". When were the other series held? I questioned. The boy replied "The Second World Cup series were held in 1979 and the Third World Cup series in 1983." I further enquired about the countries which won the same series. "West Indies won the first and the second series and the third was won by India." Very good, another question to you, in the year 1986 in Sharjah, of all the players who bowled well? "It was Maninder Singh. He took four wickets for just 22 runs". Right, in the one day matches played up till now, who scored the highest and when? "It was in the year 1983 and the match was between Sri Lanka and Pakistan. On that day nine wickets fell for 288 runs". When the boy was answering all my questions so correctly, his parents were bewildered and turned pale. The parents were silent and mum. The boy looked at me with shining eyes.

I chided the parents thus: "In this case the fault is yours, cent per cent. As a matter of fact there is nothing wrong with the boy. His memory power is great, more brilliant than ever expected. The only fault is your wrong direction. You have offered negative suggestions to him. Instead of giving positive suggestions such as, he would become a doctor or an engineer, or, if he got meritorious marks you would train him to become a great cricketer and so on, you have stated negative suggestions which spoiled his brain and ruined his future. Instead of encouraging him you have ruined him with negative suggestions. You have already done much harm to him". After that, I hypnotised him, giving him positive suggestions so as to improve his faculties in the studies also. Now the boy is getting first rank in every class. This is not a story. This is real, and a fact for all time to come.

Good Memory

It cannot be said that each and every one who is prone to loss of memory can get relief by means of hypnotism. Loss of memory can be relieved by means of hypnotism. Loss of memory may be due to damage of the brain, excessive smoking and sometimes due to much stress and strain. The loss of memory in such cases can be remedied by neuro-surgeons and neurologists. Those who are addicted to drink and those who had to work strenuously for long periods of time, after some time can become normal persons and work as usual with their normal mental faculties. A survey reveals that loss of memory or amnesia is present generally among scientists. Their minds are pre-occupied in analysing a formula or some relevant ideas concerning their research work. Their usual daily chores, taking their lunch and attending to their laboratories go on mechanically. During that time if any one questions them they cannot give appropriate answers. Sometimes they even ask the persons who approach them to repeat their questions once again, as they are wandering in their wonderlands. After hearing their questions they try to answer them in the usual fashion.

In this connection, we have to examine or view the position of reputed scientist Albert Einstein. Generally, Einstein was in the habit of thinking. Once when he was approaching his chambers in Princeton University, one of his students met him on the way. The scientist smiled at him and enquired about his wellbeing. The student replied to the scientist suitably and praised him for his memorable lectures. The student reminded him of his lunch invitation. His wish for offering a lunch remained unfulfilled. The scientist had also expressed similar wish for such a small gesture and enquired his student at which place he had actually met him (the scientist), whether he was coming from the side of the office of the Registrar. Then the scientist informed his student that he had already taken meals in the house of the Registrar and that he would certainly fulfil his wish at some other time. The scientist without looking for the answer of the student, walked briskly towards his chamber.

The usual amnesia which students experience at the time of their examinations may be cured by an expert hypnotist and by following the advice given by the hypnotist. Worries, financial difficulties in the families of students may be some of the causes for loss of memory.

One of the pre-requisites to improve one's memory is self-confidence. If one is possessing grip and determination, many things can be achieved in this world, not only memory, but many more things.

In U.S.A. the students are trained in such a way as if every one of them is going to become the President of America. The teacher and the taught are so optimistic that they can achieve whatever they wanted. Their perseverance and mental faculties are strengthened in that fashion, and so, similar mental make up and morale can be developed in others with scientific application of hypnotism.

■ ■

How to Hypnotise? 8

Hypnotism is the science of producing a calm and relaxed mental state, resembling sleep, induced by the suggestions of the hypnotist. The above state is known as hypnosis. The process is described in simplest, positive phrases, filling average human mind.

The hypnotic state is the result of coordination and cooperation between the hypnotist and the subject. When you want to hypnotise a person, see that the chair or couch used is a comfortable one and make sure that his clothes do not restrict his free movements. The light should be diffused in the consulting room and blue coloured bulb could make the subject more comfortable. If the subject desires to drink fresh water let him have it. He can also visit the bathroom for any necessity. He should at least spend an hour in the chamber to get hypnotised.

After the subject is seated comfortably in a chair or lie on a cot, close the doors of the consulting room to keep silence and then begin to hypnotise the subject. Ask the subject to close his eyes and pay attention to your voice and imagine according to your suggestions during the course of the session.

The manner in which you give suggestions is very important. Use a quiet but husky tone of voice, which leaves no doubt that you are fully confident and know what you are doing. While you are making suggestions, never make uneasy pauses. What are you saying should flow smoothly and easily. It is wiser to memorise the phrases (or put it in writing) you are going to use so that you may speak easily and fluently when attempting an induction.

You should clarify first any doubts or any fears that the subject have in regard to the science of hypnotism before you start induction, because many are reluctant to be hypnotised for no specific reasons. Therefore, convince the subject and clear the misconceptions, if any.

Some persons agree to be hypnotised but resist subconsciously. Therefore, it is necessary to repeat the hypnotic procedure until their resistance is neutralised. Explain them about the merits and benefits that the subject would gain after the therapy, to enjoy the state. The following procedure is advised to hypnotise your subject. Advise him to close his eyes and listen to your voice attentively and proceed in the following manner:—

Relax............Relax............Relax

You are going to experience a wonderful state of relaxation. Everything will be smooth and easy. Make yourself as comfortable as possible.

Relax your hands[+]

Relax your legs[+]

Relax your entire body[+]. Remove all other thoughts from your mind and continue to listen to the suggestions attentively and visualise accordingly.

Now take three long breaths that will make you relax more and more[*].

Relax your hands.......Relax your legs........Relax your entire body.......

Now imagine that your legs are getting relaxed

[+] Give time between suggestions
[*] Give time for breathing

Now imagine that your hands are getting relaxed

Now imagine that your entire body is getting relaxed

Now imagine that your legs are getting more and more relaxed

Now imagine that your hands are getting more and more relaxed

Now imagine that your body is getting more and more relaxed

Now imagine that your legs are completely relaxed

Now imagine that your hands are completely relaxed

Now imagine that your entire body is completely relaxed

Now imagine that your hands are getting heavy

Now imagine that your legs are becoming heavy

Now imagine that your body is becoming heavy

Now imagine that your hands are more and more heavy

Now imagine that your legs are more and more heavy

Now imagine that your body is more and more heavy

Now imagine that your hands are completely heavy

Now imagine that your legs are completely heavy

Now imagine that your eyelids are becoming heavy

Now imagine that your eyelids are becoming very heavy

Now imagine that your eyelids are completely heavy

Now you cannot open your eyes

The more you try, the more difficult it becomes

Now you are slowly going into sleep easily

You are very very sleepy, very very sleepy, very very sleepy

Now I am going to count the numbers from 1 to 10

With every count, you feel very very sleepy and you will be

going into deep sleep. By the time I reach number ten, you will be in deep, sound and pleasant sleep:

One — slowly you are going into sleep[+]

Two — slowly and steadily you are going into sleep

Three — now you are enjoying wonderful sleep, your body is completely heavy and completely relaxed

Four — you are going to deeper and deeper sleep[+]

Five — Now you are still going into deeper and deeper sleep

Six — ....Seven..................................

Eight — ....Nine.................................

Ten — ....

By this time, the person will be in deep hypnotic sleep and you can give him necessary suggestions prescribed to improve his health etc.

How to Terminate Sleep?

After the hypnotic sleep is experienced for a few minutes by the person, you can wake him up by giving the suggestions in the following manner.

"You have wonderfully enjoyed the relaxation, heaviness and hypnotic sleep.

Now, you are coming back to the normal condition. I shall count the numbers from 5 to 1. By the time, I call number one, you will totally come out of the trance and feel very fresh.

You feel fresh, very energetic and very enthusiastic.

Five — slowly the heaviness of your body is disappearing

Four — slowly you are coming out of the sleep

Three — the heaviness of your body has totally disappeared

+ Repeat three times

94

The Hypnotist with his subject in a hypnotic session

Two   — you have totally come out of the sleep

One   — you are very fresh, open your eyes.

Positive feelings must be suggested to the subject which will reinforce the therapeutic session. As has been said, no patient should leave the consulting room without a feeling of well being and hope.

Always give positive suggestions, never give negative suggestions. For example, say "your memory power will be increased" but never say "you will no longer suffer from bad memory" and so on.

Remember that a hypnotised subject (or person) will resist any suggestion that may threaten him in some way, real or imaginary. People have a very wide range of fears, which are highly subjective to define.

While the subject is in the trance, he will be attentively following your suggestions. Better you write those suggestions on a paper and read out to avoid any confusion. The subconscious mind should not be burdened with too many suggestions at a time.

Some of the post-hypnotic suggestions can be recorded on a tape and could be played frequently. The more often it is played to the subject, the more effective they will be. Remember however, post-hypnotic suggestions work virtually at any depth of trance and so you should not put them off.

No uneasiness should be entertained if a subject does not wake up immediately in response to your suggestions from the trance state, which will of its own accord turn into ordinary sleep in case your subject is tired. The length of time he sleeps will be dependent on how tired his body is. In this way hypnosis makes possible a degree of relaxation and recuperation which would not have been possible through normal sleep.

When you wish to wake up your subject, you have to merely suggest, "Now you are going to wake up" and then count slowly from five to one.

Upon awakening from a hypnotic trance the subject undergoes a change in consciousness. This can be described as a regaining-of-will, of memory, of reasoning powers, and, a reorientation or picking up the threads of consciousness again. The time taken to awaken varies with individuals. You will find that your subject will always come out of the trance relaxed, refreshed, feeling exceptionally well. Subjects have occasionally complained of a slight headache on awakening. This is rare and the reason for it is only due to heaviness in suggestion. Any possibility of this can be prevented by omission of such a suggestion.

Also, a suggestion should be given to the patient that he will begin to feel better and that the hypnotic experience has been a learning experience and has shown him what he can accomplish in everyday life. He should be told that on opening his eyes he will be alert, awake and ready to undertake whatever activity he wishes to, during the later part of the day, and that he will remain calm and relaxed while so doing. He will also feel good, sleep well and will awaken the following day refreshed and invigorated.

Once again, words are tailored to fit the condition for which the patient is being treated. Positive feelings must be suggested to the patient or subject earlier, which will reinforce the therapeutic session. As has been said earlier no patient or subject should ever leave the consulting room during session.

At the termination of the hypnotic session, the patient should always open his eyes with a conviction that he has taken a positive step forward towards the relief of his earlier problems

Suggestions to Hypnotists

Each science has got its own set rules, principles, ideas, a code of conduct and discipline to be adopted so as to achieve the preordained goals prescribed for that particular purpose. In the same way hypnotism, the science of hypnosis, has a set of rules and regulations and is guided by a code of conduct and discipline. It is only because of this that a person approaches a reputed hypnotist with firm belief and confidence. So, ethically his belief should not be belied by any hypnotist. The well known American Hypnotherapist Dr. Denin Flin, in his book *"The Practice of Hypnotism for patients and practitioners",* mentioned the ideals and principles which should be followed by a hypnotist, and which were acclaimed by one and all.

1. When you want to hypnotise another, first of all you should know whether you have the confidence to do. If you have mastered self-hypnotism then you can proceed — as we taste before we serve it to others — it is also the same with the hypnotist. You have to perfectly learn how to hypnotise yourself. It will infuse self confidence in you and admirably

97

put you on an even keel, when you attempt to hypnotise others.

2. Those who are ignorant of hypnotism criticise the same. If you are an experienced hypnotist, you should not get offended, but try to answer their queries and make them understand what is hypnosis and what is not. If they turn a deaf ear to your reasoning, then ignore them. One day an elderly person approached me and declared that no one could hypnotise him. Recently one hypnotist tried to hypnotise him but poor fellow failed. We should not dislike such an elderly person just for his statement. We have to assume that the so called hypnotist might not have mastered the art of hypnotism from fundamentals. The reputed hypnotist's duty is to educate such pseudo-hypnotists so that they may once again study the subject and understand things in the right perspective, so that they could help the needy, when approached in good faith.

3. When you hypnotise your subject, and when he is in a deep trance the subject may drop his head, may stiffen his hands and legs and the facial expressions may vary or change. This may happen at any stage of a hypnotic show. The audience may laugh at the subjects by observing their postures. But being a reputed hypnotist, you should not laugh. By means of showing silent signals with the help of your hands, you may silence them. If the subjects feel that others are laughing at him, he may terminate his trance-like-state (except the insane) and walk out of the show. So the practitioners of hypnotism should be very careful in this aspect and maintain the high and laudable tradition of the science of hypnosis and the hypnotic techniques.

4. Those persons who want to be hypnotised approach you and ask numerous questions. The best hypnotist should listen to all their questions with a lot of patience and answer their queries to their satisfaction. The hypnotist should not loose

his cool. If he answers even with a speck of anger, their confidence in your therapy of healing powers may dwindle and you would be losing a good opportunity. A medical practitioner may burst with anger, but the medicine which he gives to his patient will mitigate the pain or the afflictions of his patient. But patients usually approach hypnotists with psychological problems. Here the hypnotist will have to show a lot of patience, perceive the problems of the patients with sympathy and ailments or problems with compassion by giving much consolation and assurance.

You should not give the impression to your would-be-subject that you are a fresher in the field of hypnotic science. If by chance you announce it before hand, the would-be-subject would certainly leave your consulting room and would never pay a second visit. It will be proper for you to say that your hypnotic experiment will give him happiness, improve his self confidence and will bring out the hidden powers lying untouched in his unconscious mind, which is a fact.

Being a noted hypnotist you should not put on airs. In the same way you should not look down on others. If one is having an aptitude for hypnosis he or she can study books on hypnotism. There are numerous books on the subject and any enthusiast of hypnotism can study them and can satisfy their curiosity and enlighten others who are receptive to it. A number of hypnotists who canvassed for themselves that they were the top people in the said field, went behind the curtains. It is a well known fact that knowledge and education is not one's monopoly. Unnecessary criticism, advertising their egoistic tendencies and other objectionable statements will ruin them.

If you are a new entrant to the hypnotic science you better hear the case of your patient and if you want to take up, do it with as much attention as possible. If you feel that the case has to be handled by a senior hypnotist, and more so if it is a psychological case, you better advise them and recommend their case to a senior.

A hypnotist cannot try to cure physical ailments, because it is beyond his ambit. When a patient comes to you, do not get surprised nor show too much enthusiasm. At the same time, you should not remark adversely. You have to behave in such a manner as if that particular case is a familiar one to you. If not, he or she may not intimate you the full details of their case for reasons best known to them.

Very recently, a gentleman paid a visit to my clinic along with his daughter who was studying B.Sc. She was in love with a boy. It came to the notice of her parents and they did set the matter right without harming or endangering the future of their daughter. But the past event had been haunting her and she was upset. Earlier they approached another hypnotist. The misbehaviour of that hypnotist caused much worry and annoyance to the girl and to her parents. They bade good-bye to the hypnotist and left that place once and for all. So, you have to decide whether you are going to take up that case or want to refer it to a senior hypnotist or to a psychiatrist, after hearing the entire case history.

The learning of self-hypnotism is similar to that of short hand. A consistent learning of the same gives you a lot of happiness and encouragement. So practise the subject of hypnotism regularly and read the relevant books. You can keep a record of the course of treatment you have given to your patients. But keep their identity in confidence. Try to use a code like A,B, and C and so on. Either the code or the other details mentioned in your note book will be useful to you at a later stage.

The mental calibre and receptivity of suggestions cannot be the same among your patients or subjects. One subject may enter into deep trance in the first instance. But another may not be able to attain that level even after three or four attempts made by you. You should not criticise that particular subject nor reprimand him. If you chide him, you will be showing an accusing finger at his individuality. Instead of that you can convince him with patience, remove the mental block which he may be having at that particular point of time, and give suggestions so that he can enter the trance serenely.

When you hypnotise your subject, utter the words slowly and give time between suggestions. If you pronounce the suggestions rapidly, your efforts of putting them in trance may fail. Practise the art of hypnotism with great care. It is a must to have a thorough knowledge of different levels of hypnotic state, so that you can treat your patients quite adroitly and successfully.

■ ■

Self-Hypnotism 8

Any person can hypnotise himself and attain a peaceful state of mind. This is known as self or auto-hypnotism. It is also known as "auto-suggestion". Before actual science of hypnotism was made known to the world, our ancient Indians were following the technique of self hypnotism or auto-suggestion.

My belief that the usefulness of self-hypnotism was known to mankind many years ago, is based on my experiences in conducting hypnotic demonstrations during many lecture tours. Later on, my belief enhanced by witnessing the powerful effects produced by self-suggestion when the impressionable imaginations were manipulated by witch doctors and other indigenous medicine men and healers.

It (self-hypnotism) was loosely known as "*Yoga*" (*Yoga* sleep) in ancient Indian prayers from time immemorial. *Yogis* and *Sadhus* attained trance like state called "*Yoga*" in a matter of a few seconds, by controlling their minds.

In recent years the utility of hypnotism has been well recognised by various countries in the world. That too, a genuine experiment on this science gives a lot of hope and satisfaction. It has been well established by psychiatrists and hypnotherapists that mental ailments can be cured completely by means of self-hypnotism.

With self-hypnotism one can reform oneself, can rid oneself

of some bad habits, phobias, associations, inhibitions and improve self-confidence to attain many things needed in life.

There is a belief in the public that learning self-hypnotism is very difficult and cannot be acquired. By approaching a senior hypnotist, and with his guidance, one can learn it in a day. One must have a strong will, a clear mind, and an effective concentration to learn self-hypnotism. If a person can hypnotise himself by means of self-hypnotic techniques, he can continue the same to reach optimum level.

Generally to get hypnotised is akin to self-hypnotism. A subject who imagines the suggestions, usually given by a hypnotist, applies the same suggestions mentally and is able to enter the trance, a state cannot be considered as an ordinary achievement. Such a subject controls the disturbing thoughts and enters the trance. This is also equivalent to self-hypnotism. If the subject fails to control his disturbing thought pattern, he cannot enter the trance.

Let us suppose that you are thinking about a friend living in America. You are recollecting the happiest moments which you had experienced when he was in India. Naturally at that particular moment you will be forgetting your surroundings and the place where you are seated, and re-living your past events.

If any one touches you or calls you, then with a jerk you will come to your senses. It can be compared in a way to a day dreaming episode.

There are some who, while advocating hypnotherapy have questioned the therapeutic practicality of self-hypnosis.

It is the inclusion of self-hypnosis in the field of hypnotherapy that increases its probabilities of success and preserves its gains. Hypnotists have discovered that they get better results when they teach patients the technique of self-hypnosis. Cures can be permanent because the practice of self-hypnosis reinforces the therapeutic suggestions and enables the patient to repel the self-destructive suggestions of his associates and surroundings.

So, a person who is interested in self-hypnotism need not have any qualifications to learn the same. But he has to strain every nerve to study the same and practice with a discerning eye on its therapeutic value.

Principles of Self-Hypnosis

Self-hypnosis, also known as auto-suggestion, is nothing but a person hypnotising himself. It is advised to take hypnotic suggestions from an experienced hypnotist to achieve this stage. Famous Hindu saints used to meditate, slow their heartbeat, retard the body metabolism, eliminate pain etc. A student of self-hypnosis can re-shape his life, become more self-confident and motivated, eliminate fears and undesirable habits and shape himself into the person he would like to be.

The principal ingredients of self-hypnosis are relaxation, concentration (controlled attention) and visualisation.

The best way to develop these qualities is to practise them daily for a specific purpose. If you faithfully practice you will have no need of supplementary exercises of any kind.

As you practise self-hypnosis, you will discover something wonderful is happening to you and relaxation becomes a way of life. You will experience a new sense of physical awareness which will enable you to erase stress and tension from your body. Many times, during the day, you will mentally track your body from unnecessary tension and you will soon develop the knack of relaxing those tense areas instantly. You will do this silently undetected by others. Thus you will be developing a healthy tranquillity, while your associates may be reacting adversely to the same stress. After all, events are same in human history and what makes the difference is the way one reacts.

From my own experiences in *Yoga*, I came to the conclusion that the stages of the *yogic* trance and self-hypnosis are identical, if not same.

The trance, or self-induced hypnotic state, can be achieved in several ways, varying from religious ritual to a clinical hypnotic induction. It is attributed to many different causes. Some people believe it as caused by God, others by magic or spirits or just by auto-suggestion. It should be borne in mind that when one attains the state of trance, it can be used to produce diversified objectives. For instance, insensibility to pain (analgesia), single mindedness in study, a cure for some psychosomatic ailment, increased confidence, conducting research into extra sensory perception, or as in *Yoga*, to develop spirituality etc.

The student of hypnotism will find many advantages in learning self-hypnosis, for in doing so he has the opportunity of playing the dual role of hypnotist and subject, and also be able to comply the technique of self-hypnosis and auto-suggestion in his own life.

Many of you are aware of transcendental meditation propounded by Maharishi Mahesh Yogi of India. As per this system, the subject will be given a *"mantra"* or a *"beejakshara"* (the essential part of a spell or charm). After closing the eyes one can chant the *"mantra"* or the *"beejakshara"* and can enter the trance like state. Whether it is transcendental meditation, or meditation of any type the practitioner of self-hypnosis must possess concentration.

Post Hypnotic Suggestions for Self Hypnosis

It is better to give precise instructions on just how your subject is to carry out his self-hypnotic sessions. Prescribe a definite routine such as when you are about to begin a self-hypnotic session breath deeply ten times and as you do so, you will begin to feel relaxed and sleepy. If you are lying down look at the ceiling, or if you are sitting, look straight ahead and start silently counting numbers within. When you get to 'ten' your eyes will close by themselves and you will continue counting silently, getting drowsier as you continue. When you reach 'twenty' stop counting and rest, for you would have sunk down deeply to register suggestions in your unconscious mind.

Post Hypnotic Suggestions for Subject to Terminate a Self-Hypnotic Session

Make post hypnotic suggestions to your subject that he would never have any difficulty in waking himself from the hypnotic state. Prescribe some simple routine which he is to use to terminate his hypnotic sessions, such as counting backwards from 'five', and becoming wide awake at 'one'.

Some enthusiasts feel that they can hypnotise themselves. But they have to tune their minds to the suggestions as given below. It is a known fact that subconscious acts on suggestions. It is always better and more effective, to use simple and positive sentences than using compound and negative sentences, to communicate with subconscious.

(a) "I can hypnotise myself, I can enter the deep trance state. I am confident to achieve it."

(b) "By self-hypnosis my mental health certainly improves. I will be brave. I can do good things with lot of self-confidence."

(c) "I am resolute. I can surely enter the deep trance all by myself."

(d) "After the trance, I will be a happy man. I will feel fresh."

If every practitioner of self-hypnosis conditions his attitude like this, the trance like state can easily be attained without any difficulty.

106

Self-Hypnotism and Self-Analysis

In the previous chapter you have learnt how to hypnotise yourself. Now let us consider the methods of self-hypnotism which have been recognised internationally.

Practical Arrangements

See that the room in which you are conducting the hypnotic session is quiet. There should not be any interruptions at any stage. The room should neither be too hot nor too cold. There should be minimum lighting.

You can be seated comfortably making these introductory remarks. You should set apart atleast half an hour for the self hypnosis session.

Secondly, silence should be pervading the room where you are conducting the self-hypnotic session. No other sounds should disturb you. If you feel that some sounds which emanate in your surroundings may disturb your attention and concentration, better hear fine music from your tape recorder or from your radio. You should also offer a suggestion to yourself that the music may not cause any hindrance to your work on hand.

When you actually practise self-hypnosis daily for self improvement, you will soon discover what kind of visualisations works best for you.

For example, an accountant who suffered from insomnia due to worries about piled up work at the office, discovered the most helpful visualisation for him, through a little practice. In self-hypnosis, he visualised a cloth sack which he imagined contained the work which remained for him to do the next day. He visualised tying this sack tightly putting it inside a box which he closed securely and then locked the box in a large desk drawer. He visualised himself leaving the office closing the door, locking it and walking out of the office building, with a smile of relief. After practising this personalised visualisation for one week, he was able to leave his work at the office (in the emotional sense) and sleep like a baby every night thereafter. Self-improvement involves self-involvement, and the visualisations and suggestions you make will be the best ones for you.

Repetition is the main rule in making suggestions work. They should be repeated three or four times, or even more, during the day. In other words, the process of visualisation should become a habit with the practitioner.

Time must be allowed for a suggestion to be accepted by the subconscious before it is carried out. It should be put in the immediate present. To say 'My headache is gone' is contrary to the fact as it could not disappear instantly. 'My head will begin to clear soon. The ache will go away and I will feel fine', allows time for the idea to be carried out.

An example of a visual image: You are tired at the end of the day and want to overcome this by a suggestion. After suggesting that you will begin to feel refreshed, visualise yourself doing something where you are full of vigour and vitality. In your mind's eye see yourself playing golf, or tennis or some other sport, or merely walking briskly around the block swinging your arms, chest out and obviously full of pep. Carry this thought for three or four minutes. The results of such suggestions can be quite surprising in overcoming fatigue. The visual image should always represent the result desired.

Establishing a motive for acceptance of a suggestion is helpful and arousing some emotion and 'hooking' it to a suggestion will make it more effective. This may be by means of words or visual images or both, to succeed by the emotion which can be aroused easily.

Word your suggestions with only the end result in mind. Be specific about your goal. Your inner mind knows far better than your conscious mind in how to reach the goal. Stimulate it into action and it will find out the best means.

Before you begin to hypnotise yourself, analyze your needs with clarity and visualise them carefully. The answers to the following questions will help you in your decision making and guide you towards your goal. This is known as self analysis.

1. Am I losing belief in myself?

2. Is my memory decreasing day by day?

3. Am I getting angry and excited unnecessarily?

4. Am I disliking others?

5. Am I smoking too much?

6. Am I exceeding my limits while consuming liquor?

7. Do I have inferiority complex?

8. Are there any signs of obesity in me?

9. Am I criticising others for no fault of theirs?

10. Am I not congratulating others who are doing good things?

11. Am I recollecting the past moments and losing my usual moods?

12. Do I have any fears and phobias?

13. Am I getting exhausted even after doing a little work?

14. Am I feeling that I am not beautiful?

15. Am I feeling proud because I am good looking?

16. Do I have any complexes over my handicaps?

17. Am I developing anger or hatred?

18. Am I developing suicidal tendencies, relevant causes?

19. Do I feel haunted or persecuted?

20. Am I trying to hypnotise myself for the sake of fun?

If you are having more questions other than the above, you

may put those on paper. Try self-hypnosis to overcome these fears, and you shall succeed even to your disbelief.

"Every day in every way I am getting better and better" is going to be a sound piece of psychological advice for you, given by a French psychiatrist.

In the above cited questions except 19 all other questions can be answered by you if you are not having any belief in sorcery or in black magic even that will not cause you any harm. Some times that issue may not even arise.

Things like sorcery and black magic may be put off as a myth. Since they spring from your own belief. Nobody can ever have such powers, unless you have idiopathic faith in them. Because I have very close acquaintance with some black magicians, I am confidently revealing the fact.

Some Americans who are known to have such powers informed me that it is all tall-talk. Generally people go to them with some mental ailments, worries, or strong preconceived notions. They persuade them through conversation and analysis to overcome their worries and give them some talisman just to satisfy them and nothing else, they added. They are like placebos and hypochondriacs.

This is a fact. There is no colouring to this statement. There are such charlatans who are creating fear and phobia in the minds of others to serve their own ends. You need not entertain any such fear or phobia. Self-hypnotism is only the antidote to mental ailments and to psychological problems.

Mumbo-Jumbo

Burning the practitioners of black magic is no new phenomenon. Since times immemorial black magicians and the so called witches have been burnt on the suspicion that they have unusual evil powers. The truth is however different. Such people do not really possess supernatural powers, as they would

110

like the gullible public to believe. Knowledge of a few clever tricks is all what they need to convince vulnerable villagers.

I have come across as may as 200 such professional practitioners in India and abroad. Andhra Pradesh, where I have lately seen a spate of burning incidents, has its own share of practitioners, known as *Bhoota Vaidyas*, *Mantrikas* and *Murshads*. Their *modus operandi* is as follows: When a patient beset with doubts about being possessed or under the influence of black magic approaches them, these men who practise black magic (also known as witchcraft, *banamati*, *chetabadi*, *voodoo* etc.) try convincing the victim that he is the target of evil forces because of his good nature. Relatives and friends are usually to take the blame for the state they are in. What follows is a ritual where they are told to cut a lemon. The lemon bleeds and the victim is blissfully unaware that the knife blade has been smeared with the juice of the hibiscus *(mandara)* plant. Impressed by the practitioner's prowess the victim becomes a slave to superstition. He is told that his weakness lies in his goodness; that those he helps are invariably unfaithful; that he has financial problems (who hasn't); and *ad nauseum*. Exploitation is the name of the game and it takes the hapless victim very little time to succumb to sweet talk.

Is there really such a thing as witchcraft? Does the devil really obey the orders of his minions on earth? Certainly not. All such belief is rooted in blind faith. Were everybody to be perpetually plotting against one another and dying to injure one another, the rich and famous of the world would have all been eliminated by their rivals. Isn't it preposterous that you can eliminate your enemy by paying a black magic practitioner just Rs. 100! Such practitioners would have made fortunes, and would not be languishing in poverty, had their business of black magic succeeded.

Fear is what leads to take recourse to black magic. Hypnotism provides an answer in that it induces confidence in such people.

Just think of this. How can someone sitting in a graveyard possibly harm you?

Members of the Andhra Pradesh Magic Academy have waged a war against witchcraft and are all out to eradicate superstitious beliefs and expose practitioners of black magic. I have even allowed myself to be manipulated by black magic practitioners, who took a lock of my hair. Nothing has happened to me so far.

The fact that several psychiatrists are being approached by people who fear they have been possessed or are under the influence of black magic is proof enough to show that black magic is nothing but bunkum. For if black magic is what causes problems, how is it that doctors are able to find solutions? Surely, ways to combat black magic are not being taught in medical colleges!

The educated and civilised owe it to their less fortunate witchcraft-believing brethren to rid them of their misplaced belief in mumbo jumbo.

There have been instances in Telengana where clothes have set themselves ablaze, food has turned into insects and stones have fallen through RCC roofs. And the culprits have invariably been family members and not a spell cast by some imaginary person. People with roots firmly embedded in black magic and other such beliefs, look for a quick answer to their problems. On not being able to find it, and their so called saviour exposed, they resort to witch burning.

Villages are the breeding ground for such practices. Where doctors are shunned and black magic practitioners have their say, any ache or disorder is immediately attributed to black magic and another victim is added to the long list of talisman sporting patients.

Self-Hypnotism—Practical Guidelines

In the earlier chapters you have read some of practical tips and arrangements one has to make in the premises where you are going to hypnotise yourself and to analyze your requirements for visualisation and auto-hypnosis.

Now you will be introduced to the details of trancelike state and to practical guidelines to practise auto-hypnosis.

To develop skills of self-hypnosis, the following itinerary is suggested. Practice the progressive relaxation method by lying down just before you fall asleep. Do not concern yourself with prolonging of the trance state or giving constructive suggestions at this time. Try to enjoy complete relaxation. So you find yourself actually falling asleep for the night. Soon you will be able to relax so profoundly and quickly that by simply assuming a comfortable position, taking few deep breaths, closing your eyes and just thinking of relaxation, you will slip into sound sleep in a matter of four or five minutes, "relax... relax... relax." Say to yourself in the following manner. "I am going to experience a wonderful state of relaxation. Everything will be smooth and easy. It will make me as comfortable as possible."

My hands are relaxing (pause)

My legs are relaxing (pause)

My entire body is relaxing (pause) (Take three deep breaths.)

My hands are getting more and more relaxed - (three times)

My legs are also getting more and more relaxed - (three times)

Now my body is relaxing more and more

Now I am feeling very very sleepy, very very sleepy, very very sleepy

Now my eye lids are becoming heavy

My hands are also getting heavy (three times)

My legs are also getting heavy (three times)

My body is also getting more and more heavy (three times)

(Here you have to remember one important aspect. You should not entertain any idea whether you are entering the trance like state or not. At the same time you should not be diffident. You must possess a kind of confidence that you can hypnotise yourself).

"Now I am feeling very very sleepy, very very sleepy, very very sleepy. Now I am counting the numbers from 1 to 10. With every count, I feel very sleepy and I will be going into deep sleep. By the time I count number 10, I will be in deep, sound and pleasant sleep. One... Now my body is getting more and more relaxed. My eye lids are becoming heavy. Two... Now I am happy, I am feeling very sleepy. My eye lids are completely heavy. Three... Now I cannot open my eyes. Four... Now I am enjoying wonderful sleep. I am going into deeper and deeper sleep. Five... Now I am enjoying wonderful sleep. Every nerve and every muscle and every cell of my body is relaxing. And I am happy with this feeling. Six... I am feeling very fine. I am enjoying a peaceful state. I want to continue in this peaceful state of mind and body. Now I am entering trance like state. Seven... Now I am in deep trance. My mental health will be more balanced. My self-confidence also is increasing. I can do very well in my life. I am having the necessary perseverance, persistence and hard work to achieve the same. Eight... The sleep is becoming deeper. My mental health certainly improves in this condition. I am happy to be in this state. No ideas can disturb me. I am enjoying perfect happiness. Nine... Now I am enjoying complete hypnotic sleep. I can attain this state whenever I desire it. No person or sound can disturb this state of my mind. (The person or subject who is in deep hypnotic state of trance cannot be disturbed by any sound and will show little inclination

114

to such distractions. Ten... Feeling happy. I want to be in this trance like state always. The sleep is all the more getting deeper. And it is ever increasing. I have never experienced this kind of bliss before. Relax... Relax... Relax... Now I am experiencing a wonderful relaxation. I am fully satisfied with it."

The trance of self induced hypnotic state can be achieved in a variety of ways from religious rite or a clinical hypnotic induction. Some times you may have a doubt whether you have entered the trance like state by means of self hypnotism. The reason for this is, even though you are in a trance, you will be hearing some sounds, or the conversations which take place near your field of activity. These will never interfere with your trance. Just you ignore such sounds and conversations that take place around you. Every thing goes well according to your clear schedule.

Generally people are of the opinion that after the conclusion of the self hypnotic session, the subjects may feel some difficulty in reaching the normal state of activity. The hypnotists who have been recognised the world over have suggested two principles to know clearly the normal state of activity and these are "Alarm Awaking" and "Fore-head Touch".

Alarm Awakening

Before one begins the self-hypnosis session, one should indicate the duration of the session from twenty minutes to one hour according to the convenience and set the alarm of time piece accordingly. One has to take an auto-suggestion to themselves like "When I hear the alarm, I will be coming out of the trance like state and the sleep will desist, heaviness of my body will diminish, I will be attending to my normal chores as usual".

Forehead Touch

When you enter the self-hypnosis session, inform one of the members of your family to touch forehead after a period of half an hour (or one hour as the case may be). Then you will be coming out of the trance automatically. This is the best method which can be followed by any subject or an aspirant of self-hypnosis who uses the system for self-improvement.

Advantages of Self-Hypnosis

Self hypnosis is an invaluable method of treatment, for once the patient is instructed of the method he is to follow, he can administer a hypnotic or a self-suggestion as often as desired, without spending money in visiting a hypnotherapist.

When Mahatma Gandhi was in South Africa, whenever he felt exhausted and weary, he practised self-hypnotism and obtained tranquillity. He attained not only mental peace but also improved his self-confidence.

Self-hypnotism is a boon to those who are suffering from insomnia (sleeplessness). One can have relief from anger, stress and phobias. Your day and night practice of self-hypnosis will soon enable you to relax instantly. You will fall asleep quickly every night and sleep comfortably throughout the night, enjoying pleasant dreams. You will experience sleeplessness only as long as you choose to, and be able to tranquillize your mind easily.

The sleeplessness of those having financial problems, social contacts with several organisations, and connection with big business concerns may not get much relief with self-hypnotism only. Such persons have to consult medical practitioners and physiotherapists for relief and succour.

You will observe in a person who is practising self-hypnotism a kind of brilliance, lustre, vigour and respectability. Such a person will never feel weak or frustrated. Every day he will be bubbling with healthy enthusiasm. With self-confidence, he will

116

be on a victorious path. If he has to face some problems he will never be saddened. He will be bold and with self-confidence face those problems and strain every nerve to solve to his full satisfaction.

The application of hypnosis in dentistry is extensive and included in its uses are, the reduction of general anxiety and the treatment to specific fears such as fear of injections (needle phobia) and anaesthesia. With hypnosis one can produce local anaesthesia (a pain free region for a while). It may also be used for gagging and tooth grinding, for excessive salivation and for the control of bleeding during dental surgery, as well as for cases in which anaesthetics and drugs cannot be used for medical reasons.

Needle phobia is common among many. Those therapists who follow Freudian ideas will certainly find some very interesting aspects to consider in patients suffering from this fear of injections. The patient has come for dental treatment and not for an analysis. This should be left to the experienced psychiatrist. The uncovering of any repressed feelings which has led to this phobia could have dire consequences, both for the patient and the amateur analyst. The dentist, not particularly trained in psycho-analysis, might well find himself treating a major neurosis.

A patient with a needle phobia can be desensitized by the usual technique. The first step is to concentrate on the general anxiety outlined earlier and then to construct a specific list of the needle, syringe and injection procedure. The patient should be allowed to handle syringe and needle and other apparatus in the consulting room, and immediately after the appropriate desensitisation session, to convince him that he has got rid of this fear or phobia.

The present day students feel that they are losing interest in their studies and powers of concentration. Some can even observe the trembling of their hands and sweating of palms. This is all

117

due to their negative thinking. At such a juncture they have to hypnotise themselves to maintain their poise and courage with self-confidence and come out of the morass.

Another problem which the present generation students are facing is amnesia. They feel that their power of memory is decreasing and consequently the fear sets in. Such students can be guided to be hypnotised themselves, and by so doing they can improve their self-confidence and poise.

Self-hypnotism is very useful to women at the time of delivery. In the field of psychology, it probably would be too true to say that most women are affected at least occasionally with female psychological disorders such as painful or difficult menstruation (dysmenorrhoea), infertility, miscarriage and various other complications. Space prevents consideration of "more" than the "most" common, but treatment of all would be mostly on the same lines.

Dr. Check believed that menstruation difficulties are always psychological in origin, regardless of when they occur and of whether or not an organic condition is also present. Menstrual cramps may stem from several factors viz., self-punishment, identification, conflict over sex, avoidance of intercourse as a motive and especially as a result of suggestion.

The girls who have attained the age of puberty will be too shy and will be having numerous fears and phobias. A feeling of frigidity will never enter their minds if they practice self-hypnotism.

The pregnant women can expect a trouble free delivery if they improve their confidence by self-hypnotism and the consequent pains can also be mitigated.

Those women who frequent cinema houses for entertainment, and those who read novels as a matter of habit will be amenable to frigidity. Such women can safely go in for self-hypnotism and

118

in this connection they can consult a senior hypnotist for advice and treatment.

Inferiority Complex

Inferiority complex is a neurotic condition resulting from various feelings of inferiority, derived from real or imaginary, physical or social inadequacy and often manifested through over compensation in excessive aggressiveness, a domineering attitude etc. In simple words it is an attitude to underestimate one self on different parameters.

Some people feel themselves not worthy and inferior. Such feelings are a tremendous handicap for a peaceful and happy living. In all probability you may have some such feelings perhaps mild or strong.

Feeling of inferiority is based on conditional reflexes and result in a wrong perspective of self, which may cause many difficulties. A poverty complex is closely related to inferiority complex.

In this self-help book "*Psycho-cybernetics*", Dr. Maltz lays great stress on what he terms the responsibility for emotional troubles on wrong conceptions about yourself. Correcting these views will enable you to overcome the emotional problems.

Much can be accomplished by changing your self evaluation. You are what you think you are, and your subconscious carries out the ideas you have about yourself. It is virtually important to see yourself correctly. As the old philosophers have said *'know thyself, knowledge is power'* is another true adage.

Among other things physique and physical appearance is another reason for inferiority complex. Dr. Maltz is a plastic surgeon and he stresses the importance of *'appearance'*. Ugly features, deformities and the kind can be a great trouble. Dr. Maltz cites many cases where correction of these conditions by surgery brought great changes of personality. A congenital deformity can be a great source of self consciousness and feelings of inferiority. Some individuals who have been maimed in accidents may hold to these feelings, too strongly.

Many people have little or no sense of personal worth due to physical defects. Examples of these are deafness, bad vision, speech impediments, obesity, very short stature, etc. If defects are of psychological origin, they can be helped.

We need to realise that others think of us as much as we think of ourselves. A man of short stature, as an example should realise that quality is much more important than quantity. It is better to remember that your true friends will pay no heed to your stature.

Every one instinctively wishes to be loved and appreciated. The person who is physically beautiful or handsome is often so narcissistic as to be unable to give love or to have regard for others. One who has warmth and appreciation for others is a magnetic, attractive person, regardless of physical attributes or defects. A woman who regards herself less than beautiful, should be aware of the case of George Sand, noted French Writer. This woman has so much warmth and personal magnetism that young men fell in love with her when she was in her sixties and seventies. Yet she was very ugly but homely.

It is in our early years that inferiority feelings begin to develop. Parents often expect too much from their offspring. If the children fail to achieve that standard they may be scolded and reproached. The young child is scared to try something new for fear of failure. We should learn from our failures and then we may succeed the next time we try. Being scolded or punished for failure, blocks the incentive to try again.

For example let us suppose that a person is having inferiority complex. He will never admit that he is having that complex. Suppose you ask him as to why he is not moving closely in a

120

friendly manner with others. He will state, *'I am not interested in that'* or add *'I do not like to get close to people'* or he will say *'We cannot believe every one in this world'* and evades further questioning by you. One should not attempt to treat such person or persons. They have to take interest in themselves and try to remedy the defect or defects. Even though they rationalise with óthers, their inner secrets are kept to themselves. But at one point of time they have to confront with themselves, regarding the actual fact or the concealed truth.

Some questions are stated below to ascertain whether you are having inferiority complex or not and it is your duty to score marks as notified hereunder as a just and upright human being.

1. **If somebody criticises you:**
   a) You will leave the place reprimanding them (5)
   b) You will not talk to them (3)
   c) You will strongly support your view point at any cost (2)

2. **When you have to talk to new acquaintances:**
   a) You try to avoid them (5)
   b) You meet them with little interest (3)
   c) You speak to them immediately (2)

3. **When you visit a wedding function:**
   a) You try to receive the attention of one and all (2)
   b) You sit in a corner (5)
   c) You will be congratulating the important persons and leave the place immediately (3)

4. **When a stranger pays a visit to your house:**
   a) You will instruct the members of your family to tell the visitor that you are not in the house (5)
   b) You will ask the members of your family to know the particulars of the person (3)
   c) You meet the person and talk to him/her (2)

5. **While attending a meeting:**
   a) You proceed to that place well dressed (2)
   b) You will be going a round to receive the attention of all others (3)
   c) You will be attending the meeting casually or moderately dressed (5)

6. **If you are asked to take a seat on the dias in a meeting:**
   a) You aspire that some one should talk to you (3)
   b) You yourself talk to them (2)
   c) You keep on watching your wrist watch till the end of the meeting (5)

7. **When you have to talk to someone of opposite sex:**
   a) You will be talking to him or her looking at some other direction (5)
   b) You will be looking at them directly and talking to them (2)
   c) You will talk to them making oscillations (3)

8. **When others talk to you with self confidence:**
   a) You look at them with hatred (5)
   b) You congratulate them (3)
   c) You feel that it is their luck (2)

9. **When someone entrusts an important new work to you:**
   a) You do that work if you are able to do the same (2)
   b) You will bluntly say—I cannot do it (5)
   c) You will inform them that you are not doing well and avoid it (3)

10. **If you have accomplished any great thing:**
    a) You will not give any publicity to it (5)
    b) You will inform it to each and every one (2)
    c) You will be informing the same to some selected persons (3)

In scoring yourself, estimate these values and add marks accordingly. Prepare a score sheet. You are the best judge to know your traits and total your score. If the total of the marks is between 40 and 50, it means you are having symptoms of inferiority complex. If the total is between 31 and 39 you need not mind the same and there is no danger. If the figure ranges from 23 to 30 it means you are not having that complex. If the figure is between 20 and 22, it shows that you are having superiority complex, it may not serve your purpose in life. Some times you have to face dangerous situations (I have prepared this score sheet on the basis of the conclusions arrived by the association of psychologists of America).

As per the mark sheet every thing is clear to you. Now you have to find out an antidote for this. Try to remember the following aspects which will be very useful to you for any guidance in this matter.

1. "To err is human". You should not brood over the mistakes committed by you in the past. It will be alright if you don't repeat it again.

2. If you meet any person (he/she) and if that person is having some talent don't be intolerant of his ability. You have to feel that it is their fortune or luck. Every human being cannot be the same.

3. If somebody suspects you unnecessarily, do not get frustrated and vengeful. Just pity him for his ignorance.

4. If you start any work or any project and if it fails for no fault of yours, don't get disheartened. You make another attempt. After all one does not change the objective, but one has to change the strategies to achieve it. Remember failures are opportunities.

5. If you are having physical defects, do not give much attention to them. They will never be an impediment to achieve your

123

goal. Read about Hellen Keller? You will know how they have turned their defects into victory.

6. Your dress habits and your gait are matters very personal of yourself. You should assess yourself on what others think of you. You can follow your way of thinking, viewing the matter without other's concern and more so with self confidence.

Remember the points mentioned above. Formulate some positive suggestions as per your wishes and put it in writing. Memorise those suggestions and self hypnotise yourself accordingly. Within a month you will be noticing a great improvement in yourself and you will be happy for the change you have ushered into your life.

■ ■

Smoking 10

S ome of the books dealing with hypnosis have reported its use as a means of stopping smoking. If you are a smoker and wish to quit, some of the ideas about giving up that habit will make an helpful reading.

To stop smoking habit under normal conditions is an easy matter. But hypnosis can indeed be of great help. Those who are having firm belief in hypnotism and those who can hypnotise themselves can turn out to be non-smokers. Those who are endowed with self confidence can stop smoking forever.

Every one of us have some problems in this world. Resorting to alcoholism, drug addiction and smoking do not solve these problems. The people who watch movies and read novels give vent to such notions. According to the principles of medical science, smoking does not produce or give any mental peace or solace. Some smokers are addicted to frivolous phobias. Those who have lost self-confidence in this respect are amenable to such phobia and hence they believe that smoking energises their nerves, lessens their fatigue and invigorates their bodies. The conference of psychologists held in San Fransisco fully discussed this aspect and declared unanimously that it was a myth. The World Health Organisation (WHO) which held a meeting in Geneva in 1978 studied the habit of smoking in detail. The WHO stated that ten lakh people die every year in the world because of smoking. According to their findings 90% of lung cancer patients are dying and they are smokers. About 25% of smokers die of heart attacks and those smokers who were afflicted with diseases form 75%. So in 1980 the WHO has given a slogan: *Smoking or Health, Choice is Yours, You are wasting money and time when you buy and smoke a cigarette.*

The lung cancer and chronic bronchitis are some of the signposts for stopping smoking. Tobacco, alcohol and drug addicts should observe this and abstain from such habits not only for their good health but also for the betterment of their families. Tobacco contains upto three percent nicotine, a good reason to stop smoking. In Britain one smoker dies every five minutes. About five percent of cigarette smoke is carbon monoxide, the same stuff that billows out of car exhausts. The yellow-brown smoke in cigarette smoke causes cancer in some animal as found in experimental research. So why dribble it down your throat and into your lungs? If you smoke twenty cigarettes a day, you will be shortening your life by five years.

Dr. Henry Miller says, 'The evidence is now inconvertible that the cigarette is the main cause of the present epidemic of lung cancer.'

A woman should give up smoking for her own sake, and the desire to have a healthy child demands that she gives up smoking during pregnancy. It harms the foetus, and spontaneous abortion is more common. The mortality rate is high and the birth rate is low. They baby will be born weighing less than it ought to be and there are more deaths during the first week after birth.

The Royal College of Physicians are of the opinion that the infants and young children whose parents smoke, get more chest infections and pneumonia than those whose parents do not smoke. By the age of eleven the children of smoking mothers tend to be shorter, clumsier and less good at reading and will probably be smokers themselves in two years.

Dr. Miller states thus "Smoking causes peripheral vascular disease, or construction of the arteries of the arms and legs, which sometimes leads to permanent damage and eventually amputation".

The habit of smoking first starts as a fashion in the company of like minded friends, then develops into a regular habit. In the long run they will loose their health and will be mentally sick because of this unwanted habit.

In recent times, women are also attracted towards smoking. The Indian women belonging to higher strata of society do smoke and they feel equal to men in all respects in a male dominated society.

You may question then how anyone can get rid of the smoking habit. The smoking habit can be discontinued by means of self-hypnosis or hypnotic-suggestion.

How to Stop Smoking

A cigarette has fire at one end and a fool at the other
—Samuel Johnson

Everyone who smokes knows it does no good to them in the long run. So does heavy drinking. But the fact and reason seldom enlighten people when they seek momentary "kick" in the form of pleasure and amusement. The warning given as a ritual on the cigarette packet is passed off as a joke.

In Britain alone for instance, some 123,000 million cigarettes are made each year, earning the Government more than 2,000 million pounds a year by way of tax, and similar is the case of alcohol.

Inspired by the theme of World Health Day in 1980 "Smoking or Health, the Choice is Yours", many countries have started anti-smoking campaign with force.

In Austria, a "Gentleman's Agreement" was established between the Ministry of Health and the tobacco companies,

127

whereby the nicotine and tar content of cigarette must be indicated on packages.

In Bahrain, tobacco advertising is banned on radio and television and smoking is prohibited in school clubs.

Belgium has prohibited cigarette vending and free distribution of cigarettes. Health warnings must be placed on cigarette packets in French and Flemish. Advertisements have been banned on television, radio and cinema.

In Brazil, the tax on sales of cigarettes is now higher than that of any other consumer product, providing 12 percent of the overall Federal tax yield. A national anti-smoking programme has been established and smoking has been banned in all offices of the Health Secretariat.

Doctors in Bulgaria have been urged to give up smoking to set an example. And smoking has been banned in areas where pregnant women and nursing mothers are present.

In Canada, a nationwide 'Wheedles Wednesday' is staged each year to alert the public to the smoking hazard.

China has launched a major anti-smoking campaign with the support of the Vice-Minister of Public Health.

Restrictions on smoking in public places and ban on tobacco advertisements are in fore in Netherlands, Saudi Arabia, Singapore and United Arab Emirates, Denmark, Egypt, Finland, Greece, Iraq, Ireland, Kenya, and Sri Lanka.

India does not figure in the list of nations that have launched the anti-smoking campaign till 1981 as per the information received by the World Health Organisation. People normally start smoking for numerous reasons, like the desire to appear manly or sophisticated or out of boredom. Then smoking becomes a part of their life-style or they become addicted to the nicotine in cigarette (nicotine is one of the most addictive substances) and they cannot give up the habit.

The habit of smoking is considered to be harmful by one and all. There is a definite link between smoking and lung cancer, heart disease and chronic bronchitis. Besides, heavy smokers wrinkle faster and smell bad.

The number of tobacco users is growing very rapidly. In our country tobacco is smoked not only in cigarettes but also in the form of *bidi, cheron* and *dhunti*. It is also chewed as a ingredient of *paan* by mixing with lime and areca nut. In whatever form it is used, tobacco has the same deadly affect. It claims over 6,00,000 lives in India each year.

The inhalation of smoke that emanates from other people's cigarette is called "passive smoking". This is not only unpleasant but also harmful. A recent study in Japan has shown that the wives of smokers face the risk of lung cancer more than those of non smokers.

There seems to be only one successful approach to eliminate the habit of smoking. That is, to make up your mind firmly that you not only are going to be an ex-smoker but also what you can do about it. That without a shadow of doubt, you are stronger than an infernal weed and so you are no longer going to be its slave and that time has now come when you will no longer smoke. With this determination some will find it easy to stick to their resolution. Others will have more difficulty but will ultimately break their habit. Auto-suggestion under hypnosis can ease this process. This should include the impression in the subconscious mind the reasons for stopping. Positive suggestions to minimise the desire to smoke, should be made. It is a mistake to suggest no desire at all, for there is bound to be some craving.

You better suggest to your smoker friend to make a formal contract with himself and to take a firm decision to stop smoking. All he has to do is to tell himself that the will stop smoking on such and such a day. Let the period be three days or a week. To prove his firm decision, he has to observe the following principles in the first instance.

1. He has to inform his friends and his relatives that he would not be smoking from three days, or a week hence. Let that day be known as "Quit day".

2. He should try to be as busy as possible till the 'Quit day.' He has to keep aloof from the company of smokers. If he wants to smoke before the Quit day advise him to smoke only half of the quantity which he used to smoke previously. Ask him to put the butts in the ash-tray and not to clean it for he should know how many cigarettes he had smoked.

3. According to the psychologists, to improve one's self-confidence one has to bathe in hot water immediately followed by lukewarm water. Ask your patient to take such baths so that he will be able to control his mind and improve his self-confidence considerably. This method should not be followed by those who are a bit unwell or suffering from any other ailment.

4. He should not entertain any feeling that his friends may gibe if he is going to avoid smoking. Advise your subject to smoke with his left hand (if he was using right hand previously) or if he is left handed, ask him to smoke with his right hand till the Quit day arrives.

5. As the quit day approaches the patient would be feeling more happy that he would be giving up smoking soon. To avoid the desire to have a smoke, advise him to drink a glass of water, or any fruit juice. These are useful and beneficial to his body and to maintain a good health.

6. The thought that smoking is important for maintaining good health and keeping him fresh all through the day is a myth. It is simply a phobia and therefore advise your patient to give up that phobia and be a positive non-smoker soon.

7. Advise him not to buy cigarette till the Quit day, if possible. He has to take a firm decision to that effect. If need be, a

substitute may be taken to satisfy the craving, such as chewing gum, a fruit or peppermint drops.

8. Ask your patient to visit your consulting room on the appointed day, i.e. the Quit day without fail. Even if you (the hypnotist) are a smoker, do not smoke in the presence of your patient. When your patient observes all the do's and don'ts mentioned above, it will be easy for you to prepare him for a trance-like state and Aversion Therapy can be utilised optimally for better results.

Hypnotherapy, drug therapy, and counselling are some of the methods to quit the habit of smoking. The first two, hypnotheraphy and drug therapy are yielding the best results in our country.

Hypnotherapy to Abstain from Smoking

Hypnotism and auto-suggestion can greatly aid in minimising the desire to smoke and in strengthening one's determination.

As a hypnotist, you can advise your patient to fix the "Quit day" some fifteen days hence. He has to reduce the number of cigarettes day by day and on the quit day he has to smoke just one or two cigarettes only. During this period of fifteen days you have to hypnotise your patient three or four times to get him adjusted to the idea of reducing the number of cigarettes he usually smokes.

You have to make the patient get used to your voice and your way of giving suggestions in this regard. If you do this before the Quit day it would be easier for him to enter in deep trance. The well known psychiatrist and hypnotherapist, Dr. Rozar Baruhard of New York had formulated some suggestions and these were approved and mentioned hereunder.

"You are now enjoying a wonderful state of relaxation, now I am counting from number 1 to 10. Each number will take you a step close to deep trance. One ....you are now more

131

motivated and more determined than ever before to reject all the bad habits that are harmful to you. You will be entering a still deeper trance state. Two.........your entire body is completely relaxed. You are feeling very very sleepy and your eyelids are becoming heavy. Three.....Four.....Five.....Six.....Seven..... Eight.....Nine......Ten...... . Now you are in a fully hypnotic state of sleep".

Give a pause and again continue your suggestions like this "Till I suggest anything to you, you will be enjoying and experiencing a wonderful state of sleep".

Give a pause and again continue your suggestions like this "you now reject this habit of smoking cigarettes. You have all the right reasons to be a non-smoker. You do it for yourself, for your health and well-being and that feeling's fine, the feeling's fine".

"You are now taking a most important decision with a lot of confidence and this will create a new image for you, change your usual habits and you will have good health and you will be alert. You are waiting to see that enchanting moment. You are rejecting once and for all the habit of smoking which has been troubling you all these years. You have made up your mind, you have made the choice to be a non-smoker and that feeling is fine, the feeling is fine. Your body now rejects smoking. Your lungs no longer want those poisonous fumes in them, they now want to become clean and cleaner and healthy once again".

"Your senses feel clean and fresh. You have made up your mind to start a new life, which is healthy and enjoyable. You are now very near to that state of healthy life" (if need be, send your patient to a deeper trance state to achieve better results).

"You are now experiencing a wonderful state of relaxation. You have been addicted to smoking cigarettes having nicotine which is poisonous. You have continued to smoke all these years, even if it is poisonous because of nicotine. Even though you

132

know it is dangerous and poisonous you have patronised it. You were under the impression that smoking stimulates your nerves. The deceptive pleasure of the same made you think like that. If cigarettes have the quality of energising the nerves, the doctors must have prescribed the same to those suffering from nervous diseases. If so, medicine is unnecessary for them. So your feeling that by cigarettes your nerves will be energized, is simply a fallacy and nothing else. Your craving for smoking made you believe in that. You want to cover up your weakness".

"You have made up your mind to stop smoking. Your body now rejects cigarettes. The less you smoke the better you feel. Soon you will begin to notice that every aspect of your life is going to improve more and more day by day. You are having full control over your body. You are a very very important member of your family".

"You show your affection towards every member of your family. You love them, you are for them and they are for you." (As a hypnotist you should know at the beginning of the therapy the names of the members of the family of your patient). "Your family members show their affection towards you in abundance. Their affection is more important, more precious, more valuable than those cigarettes which are burning your physical frame, your nerves, your body, those cigarettes are destroying your nervous system and making you sick. Smoking endangers your life itself. Your life is more precious not only to you but also to your wife, to your sons and daughters" (here make some cigarette's smoke reach your patient, you can observe a noticeable change in his face. He will be having cough when he inhales smoke. Noticing such symptoms in your patient, hypnotise him to send him to a deeper trance-state, by giving more suitable suggestions.)

"The smell of cigarettes is now disgusting and the taste is unappealing and unappetizing. You are now a non-smoker and the feeling is wonderful. In future if any one offers you a cigarette

Hypnòsis as a substitute for anaesthesia

you would be rejecting it. Thus in future you would be keeping aloof from nicotine" (if need be, give him more suggestions to achieve best results).

If you hypnotise him three or four times before the Quit day (once in three days) your subject will never smoke. Continuation of such hypnotic sessions will depend on the nature of the patient.

Finally, as a hypnotist of repute, you have to mention it to your patient thus "Maintaining your health is now in your hands. Now it is left to you, whether you are going to maintain perfect health or destroy the same to the annoyance or dismay of the members of your family who are sincerely and affectionately wishing you the best of health".

Give necessary instructions to your patient in self-hypnotism and offer relevant suggestions. Then your patient will obviously be on the path of maintaining good health to the satisfaction of the members of his family. ■ ■

How to Overcome Stress

*"On earth there is nothing great but man; in man
there is nothing great but mind"*
– Sir William Hamilton

The nature or content of mind determines how and what organs of the body will receive and the kind of response that will be made. Constructive thoughts directed to the accomplishment of a goal or strongly held objectives stimulate and integrate all body processes. Thinking, incited by situations of fear, doubt, anxiety and frustration has a debilitating effect upon health and normal well-being.

It is recognised by outstanding medical authorities that not less than 75% of all cases of ill health are due to mental and emotional problems.

Malignant tumours constitute a threat to health and life for a significant segment of our population. There are some authorities who believe that cancer is the result of a misdirected emotional drive. Certainly we are living in an age of stress.

While certain types of stress such as the stress caused by a romantic encounter or the anticipation of a reward can do good to you, stress that begins to produce depression is completely undesirable.

If you are a lady, you may experience stress as a product of premenstrual syndrome (PMS). Current estimates show that out of 33 to 50 per cent patients of America, women between the ages of 18 and 45 years experience premenstrual syndrome (PMS). This amounts to ten to fifteen million women. The emotional symptoms include confusion, temporary memory loss, and mood swings from euphoria to despair. Here again, proper nutrition can be of great help and the addition of B Complex Vitamins ease the symptoms. When dieting programmes are followed along with hypnotherapy, PMS can be greatly reduced, if not eliminated entirely.

The four words, calmness, composure, control and confidence are repeated to the patient as frequently as possible so that these qualities become a conditional response to the problems which the instructor will subsequently deal.

The mental stress is being discussed everywhere and people interpret it in many ways. It can be mitigated by self-hypnotism and *Yoga* (*yogasanas*). In the present day world the human being is in a way subjected to many aspects of stress because of financial issues, social problems, family burdens, etc.

A housewife, while she is preparing the children to school, gets disturbed when the calling bell rings. The barking of the dog in the house, the quarrels of the children among themselves, the unexpected absence of the servant etc. add to her troubles and she is subjected to a great deal of mental stress.

Stress is even greater for office going people. The work burden in the office, the boredom which the employees experience in the office hours make them feel exhausted. When they return to their home the ladies begin their stories or woes. Expecting such a situation, the husbands glance through the newspaper just to avoid the annoyance on the home front, while music emanating from the radio reaches the ears as a back ground lullaby.

Dr. Edward Charles Worth has recently conducted a survey among the students of Ballers College of Medicine and the findings are as follows.

Every year a million people are afflicted with pain in the heart. Thirty million people are subjected to blood pressure. Tumours in the abdomen have been noticed in eight million people. Twelve million people are prone to drinking habit. Millions of people are gulping sleeping tablets to mitigate their diseases and mental worries.

But you need not feel perturbed over the statistics if you remember nine golden rules to reduce stress, they are:

1. One should not view that life itself is an issue. Life is something like a play, a game. One can solve all the issues with a smile. If one faces the difficulties with a "smile" on, there will be thrill in it.

2. Prepare a planned procedure and follow it strictly or else there will be stress on your veins. You have to write it on a paper what all you have to do during that day and divide it under three headings:

   i) Very very important

   ii) Very important

   iii) General

   If you follow as per the headings, keeping in view the time available, you can spend all the time in a happy way without fussing and fretting.

3. Unfortunately those who belong to physically retarded or handicapped segment, feel that they have failed in their lives. Entertaining such ideas is utterly a mistake. Hellen Keller was blind, deaf and dumb. Those impediments never kept her indoors. With self-confidence she conducted research and became a renowned scientist.

4. Don't show aversion or resentment to others who occupy high places in life. What is required is simple living and high thinking, higher goals to achieve in your life. Limit your

wants and live happily with members of your family with contentment.

5. Don't burden yourself with the problems of others on compassionate grounds. If you could not solve their problems as promised, you have to bear the brunt of it. Your stress will be greater than ever before, as you have to attend to your own errands.

6. You have to improve your mental composure. Those who are jealous of your capability or those who criticise you for no fault of yours, pity their outbursts and look at them compassionately. It gives you a lot of mental satisfaction and improves your image in the eyes of the public.

7. Try to complete the work on hand punctually before you begin another work. Pending completion of the earlier one, and to concentrate on the second work may lead to stress.

8. Lead a contented life. Greed leads you nowhere. We can have many examples from the pages of history to quote. The lives of Napoleon I (Napoleon Bonaparte : 1769-1881), the French Emperor; Adolf Hitler (1889-1945), the Nazi dictator of Germany during 1933-1945, are some such examples. You know much about Hitler. He was greedy and had no contentment in his life time. He had no mental peace. He could not sit at one place even for just ten minutes. Finally he committed suicide.

9. The last but not the least is — making a compromise with the prevailing circumstances. If we persist in our deals, we have to face defeat and dismay.

These are the nine excellent rules one may like to know and to practise them. Such persons can also approach a hypnotist and seek guidance.

One must be brave, bold and face any situation with courage and fortitude.

Methods of Relaxation

Relaxation means relaxing or being relaxed, a loosening or lessening of severity, a lessening of or resting from work, worry of effort, and recreation of other activities for bringing this about.

Accompanying nervous tension is the inability to relax. Chronic tension is most detrimental to both physical and mental well-being and often a main cause in producing psychosomatic illnesses such as stomach ulcers for example. Relaxation tends to discharge nervous tension, at least temporarily. With practice in relaxation, chronic tension could be overcome to a larger extent.

Several books have been written on the techniques of relaxation. Best known of these is Jacobson's 'You must relax', a self-help book which was published in 1924. It is now out of print. However for the benefit of the readers, the Jacobson's relaxation technique is given here.

Dr. Edmund Jacobson developed Progressive Relaxation during the 1920's while working with patients suffering from chronic muscle tension and anxiety. He asserted that the body responds to anxiety-provoking thoughts and events with muscle tension, which actually increases the subjective experience of anxiety. He found that deep muscle relaxation reduced physiological tension and was incompatible with anxiety. Progressive-relaxing-muscles also lowered blood pressure, pulse, respiration, and perspiration.

Progressive Relaxation teaches you to sense and then relax each set of muscles. As you study these exaggerated movements, you become more aware of tension signals. Soon you learn that relaxation is just the opposite of tension, no signals, no holding, and no motion. Progressive Relaxation does not require imagination, will-power, or suggestion. All you must do is contract them, let go of tension in each mat or muscle group in your body.

How to Relax

These instructions include a long and a short version. You may want to make an audiotape of the long version to replay when you first learn the technique. If you do tape, pause for about ten seconds after giving a command to tense, and atleast twenty seconds after giving a command to relax. When you are thoroughly familiar with the long version, you may want to memorize the short version in which you can simultaneously tense and relax many muscles at once, to achieve deep muscle relaxation in a very brief time.

Both the long and the short versions begin in the same way. Sit or lie down with every part of your body comfortably supported. The ideal position for this exercise is to lie flat on the floor on a mat or blanket with your hands at your sides, palms up, and your legs straight and slightly parted. A pillow under your knees may help to flatten your back. A pillow beneath your head is optional. Close your eyes and breathe rhythmically from your diaphragm.

The Long Version

Beginning with the right hand, make a fist, bend your wrist, then bend your elbow toward your shoulder. Clench your right fist tighter and tighter, studying the tension in your hand and arm. Now relax, letting your arm fall loosely onto the floor. Feel the looseness in your right hand and arm and feel the contrast with the tension. Straighten the fingers of your right hand, stiffening your wrist and elbow. Feel the tension.... then release it. Roll your arm inward until the back of your hand touches your body. Hold the tension. Now release your shoulder muscles. Roll the right arm outward, palm up, and hold the tension. Now release. Turn off all the power in the right arm.

Now repeat with your left hand. Make a fist, bend your wrist, then bend your elbow toward your shoulder. Clench your

140

left fist tighter and tighter, studying its tautness as you do. Now relax your arm. letting it fall loosely onto the floor. Notice the looseness in your left hand and arm and how it feels different from the tension. Straighten the fingers of your left hand, stiffening your wrist and elbow. Feel the tension . . . . then release it. Roll your left arm inward until the back of your hand touches your body. Hold the tension. Now release the shoulder muscles. Roll your left arm outward, palm up. Hold the tension. Now release it. Turn off all the power in the left arm.

Now turn your attention to your right leg. Curl your toes under, push your foot and ankle downward, and tense the entire leg....tighter.......tighter. Now relax. Notice the difference between tension and relaxation. Now point the toes of your right foot back toward your knee, stiffen your knee, and straighten your leg. Hold that tension. Now release it. Roll the right leg inward and tense. Now relax. Roll the right leg outward and tense. Now relax. Turn off the power in your right leg.

Now focus on your left leg. Curl your toes under, push your foot and ankle downward, and tense your left leg....tighter......tighter. Now relax. Notice the difference. Now point the toes of your left foot back toward your knee, stiffen your knee, and straighten your leg. Hold that tension. Now release it. Roll the left leg inward and tense. Now relax. Roll the left leg outward and tense. Now relax. Turn off the power in your left leg.

Slowly scan each arm and leg. Are they relaxed? As your muscles relax, they soften and lengthen. With your eyes closed, continue to breath rhythmically from the diaphragm.

Squeeze your buttocks together....tighter....tighter. Now relax. Pull in your abdomen and flatten your back to the floor. Hold the tension. Now release it. Pinch your shoulder blades toward the spine.........tense. Relax. Roll your shoulders forward toward your chest. Hold it. Now let go.

Scan your arms, legs and torso for tension. Tense and then relax any area that is not relaxed.

Turn your attention to your neck. Tuck your chin in toward your chest and hold it there. Now relax. Turn your head to the right as far as your can......hold it. Now let it return to centre and relax. Turn your head to the left as far as you can.....hold it. Now let it return to centre and relax. Push your head back into the pillow.....hold it. Now let go.

Now focus on your head. Raise your eyebrows, wrinkling your forehead and scalp....tighter. Now relax. Frown.....hold it. Let go. Squeeze your eyelids tightly together......tighter. Relax. With your lids lightly closed, turn your eyes to the right....to the left.....up.....down.....and then relax. Squeeze your jaws together. Release. Purse your lips. Relax. Open your mouth as wide as you can and stick out your tongue. Hold it. Now relax. Push your tongue against the roof of your mouth.....harder. Now let go. Swallow and relax.

Continue to breathe slowly, deeply, and regularly. Scan your body, focusing on feelings of relaxation. Your right arm..... left arm..... right leg.....left leg...... buttocks..... abdomen..... shoulders..... neck..... face..... mouth..... scalp. Quietly let the tension dissolve and let the muscles become smooth and soft. Feel calm, rested, and alert as you prepare to return to the activities of your daily life.

You need to practice this exercise for at least twenty minutes daily. You may want to divide it into two 10-minute periods. With persistent practice, you can learn to relax your entire body in a few minutes.

Be careful when you tense your neck and shoulders. Excessive tightening can cause muscular or spinal damage. If you over-tighten your toes, legs, or arms, you may experience some muscle cramping.

Pierce called his relaxation exercise "decubitis". According to him, if a group of muscles, such as an arm or a leg is tired, distraction of attention from them brings automatically complete relaxation of these muscles.

Another technique helpful in overcoming nervous tension is the practice of deep breathing. It can be combined very nicely with Pierce method of relaxation.

Yoga practitioners have found breathing exercises of great value. They believe them to be of utmost importance in maintaining health. Such breathing fills you with oxygen and clears your lungs. You feel much more relaxed and invigorated.

Yogis used the term *prana* for life force of primal energy and believed that with this exercise a fresh supply of *prana* is accumulated in the tissue and lungs. Oxygen is a part of *prana*. In theory this stimulates the entire nervous system, the body and the senses.

Yoga teaches a way of healing based on intense concentration (developed only with much practice) and then the use of auto-suggestion following this breathing exercise. However, the exercise is continued to a point of heavy perspiration and exhaustion. It is supposed to be done in the sunlight and also in the water while bathing, and with much repetition.

A better understanding of your emotions and a different view point towards some of them should be helpful to you. You can learn to modify and control them. Self-hypnosis and auto-suggestion will aid greatly in this. As you practice self-hypnosis you will certainly find that you are more relaxed and free from tension in your daily life. But if you have much difficulty in relaxing, you should practice "Pierce" method. In turn this will help you to go into deeper hypnosis. In fact, this method of relaxation has been used as a technique to induce hypnosis. Adding some suggestions to it will increase the tendency. When it is practised, some people find themselves spontaneously in hypnosis when they have concluded their exercise.

If you take time to practise breathing exercise once a day, or better twice, you will soon notice that you are feeling much better and more energetic. It aids to promote good health and is certainly worth the few moments of time needed to go through it.

The psychologists have agreed long back that a patient can have mental peace by means of hypnotism.

As a hypnotist, when a person approaches you for advice, give a patient hearing to his problem. As far as possible let him explain all his worries. You can put in a question or questions as and when necessary, prepare a case history of the patient with details of his name, age, whether married or not, symptoms of his/her disease, details of his/her employment, and details of the mental ailments in the heredity. You can hand over a question paper, if it is necessary and ask them what type of improvement or change they are aspiring for. Make it certain that their ailments should not be of a physical nature. You should begin your treatment only after ascertaining that fact.

After receiving the answers from the patients, if you want to collect some more information and record for future reference, pertaining to their daily routine, association with their friends, atmosphere in their family circles, the patient's views regarding his/her brothers and sisters, information regarding their lives, affairs, eduction, information regarding their addiction to narcotics, their views about their parents etc. tell your patients that they have to inform you the necessary particulars and details without any inhibition. Plainly inform them that they will be the sufferers if they conceal any information.

After ascertaining the fact that your patients have improved their confidence in you and in your way of treatment, you can

144

then start the treatment by putting your patients into a trance by advising them to close their eyes and listen to your voice attentively and proceed in the following manner by mentioning; "Relax... Relax... Relax.... you are going to experience a wonderful state of relaxation.... . You are feeling very very sleepy, very very sleepy, very very sleepy. Now I am going to count the numbers from 1 to 10 with every count you feel very very sleepy and you will be going into deep sleep. You are now feeling happy, very very happy. A new power, a new energy is now entering your body. In view of this new energy all your problems and worries will be solved.[+] You have to solve all your problems with intelligence for which you are known by the members of your family, by your friends, by your associates, etc. In future you will not be having any problem. You can live with contentment. You can make your life happy because you are having a built-in mechanism, the necessary self-confidence which you are now having in good stead".[*]

Stammering and Stuttering

This is a habit usually acquired in early childhood and may be due to anxiety. A small boy may be frightened of his father, of his teacher and indeed of the world. He is "struck dumb with fright".

Often the stammer will disappear as the child matures, gains confidence and is able to assert himself. When this does not occur, treatment may be sought in early adult life by which time the difficulty is firmly established. Nevertheless relaxation, through exploration and discussion of early problems and relationships together with the rehearsal of normal speech under hypnosis, offer hope and relief. In the latter phase the patient is

---

+ Here you can mention their problems and other mental observations.

* You may add some more useful suggestions here to solve their other problems keeping them in trance-state till the stipulated time of hypnotic session.

asked to repeat aloud (whilst in hypnosis and completely relaxed) a rapid succession of words which normally have proved difficult, followed by sentences from a book or newspaper. Subsequently in hypnosis the therapist should find out the role of the boss or the teacher or some authority figure in the patient's life who could cause him to stammer, and a discussion should follow showing the patient that he can speak normally in this situation. In this way the patient is desensitised to his fear of speaking.

We as speech clinicians have many reliable techniques we can use to facilitate the fluency of individuals who stutter.

Characteristics of Stammering

According to R. McDonald Ladell, stammering is a neurosis, and that inevitably has its roots in childhood. Stammering results from an internal conflict between conscious and sub-conscious urges, a conflict which has its origins back in early childhood when during his formative years the sufferer, perhaps through parental suppression, was not allowed to assert his personality, and instead became shy and developed a basic urge to keep silent. Feelings of inferiority may well have imprinted themselves on the unconscious mind and the stammering adopted as a childish defence mechanism...

Although McDonald Ladell was not a speech therapist he contributed commendable suggestions and observations to help the stammerers. The following points suggested by him may be useful to the hypnotherapists.

- Stammering is not due to organic defect, but is an emotional reaction.

- Stammering is the result of inferiority complex.

- Fear has a direct effect on the speech faculty. An individual may be in a state of chronic fear owing to a sense of inadequacy acquired in the childhood.

146

- People stammer in situations which make feel inferior.

- The first essential to cure is to learn to relax which lessens anxiety.

- Women who stammer are very few compared to men.

- Parents must examine themselves as to how far they are responsible. They should be patient with a stammerer.

- Some stammerers can cure themselves because they are situational stammerers.

- Hypnosis may positively help the stammerer to overcome his problem.

- Stammerer can speak well, sing well at home. He stammers only when he speaks to strangers, opposite sex people, over phone etc.

Fluency

When we use the term fluency, we generally mean that speech flows smoothly and continuously. By disfluency we normally refer to some form of break in that smooth flow of speech. The breaks that we most notice and come to regard as stuttering, involve a lack of smooth transition between speech sounds and a disruption in their normal sequence.

Non-stutterers also have disruptions in the flow of speech. This normal disfluencies tend to be characterised by interjections such as uh, er, ah, well, and, you know. The majority of speech disruptions produced by stutterers differ in type from the majority produced by nonstutters.

Characteristics of Stuttering

Disfluencies that tend to characterise stuttering are perceived at the articulatory level, they include (1) repetition of sounds and syllables such as *ba . . . . . .ba. . . . . .ba. . . . . .baba.* (2) unusual pauses between sounds and syllables, typically associated with prolongations or repetitions of articulatory gesture, more commonly referred to as "blocks". A block typically involves obstruction of air flow, usually accompanied by abnormal increase in tension and/or incoordination in the articulatory or laryngeal muscles.

During stuttering, vowel duration is often shortened as well. The children of ages 2 or 3 usually produce particular types of disfluencies almost frequently, part of a word, repetitions and single syllable word repetitions.

As far as children are concerned more attention should be directed to their speech at an early age. Or else, they may be frustrated in their attempts to communicate. They may also develop inferiority complex in the long run. As children spend time in social engagements outside the immediate family, they experience negative feelings which often damage their self image. The stutterer is reacting normally to the stress and severity of the communicative handicap.

Stutterers usually state that they have no control over the speech mechanism. Stutterers further add that they are embarrassed, frustrated and are humiliated by their stuttering. Some feel angry and frustrated with themselves. There is a tendency for personal problems, common to all human beings, to become associated with the speech disturbance.

The school age stutterers begin to experience these feelings and frustrations. The speech clinicians must pay attention to the stutterer's feelings, beliefs, attitudes and goals as well as to specific behavioural techniques, to increase fluency of speech in their therapy programme.

The exact cause of stuttering is not known. The current research supports a complex integration of genetic and environmental factors. The neurological susceptibility is inherited and forms the basis of most cases of stuttering.

The research conducted till recently supports the idea that stuttering susceptibility is transmitted from one generation to another with females being more amenable to the stuttering than males. If one parent has ever stuttered, the risk of stuttering increases significantly in all children, male and female, although the female still tend to be more resistant than the male. In addition to heredity, primary factors that seem to influence the development of the habit include environmental stress and an early history of speech or language difficulty other than stuttering, the latter which may reflect a disturbance on cerebral integration and/or coordination.

It usually develops between the age of 2 and 6 years. Although it may develop in later childhood, this period between 2 and 6 years is the time in which the child is developing a complex communicative system.

Stuttering children will tend to repeat parts of words, sounds, or syllables more often than nonstutterers, who will tend to repeat words and phrases more frequently.

Further research suggests that stuttering is more often linked with stressed words and with words appearing in the first part of the sentence. If the stutterer is excited or feels hurried, these factors will tend to increase stuttering whether the pressure is self imposed or imposed by some one else.

The stuttering should be considered not as a unitary disorder as it has been in the past, but as a disorder with a variety of component areas in which breakdown may occur.

We have long been aware that increased stress or anxiety tends to increase the frequency of stuttering. Often parents report that the child stutters more when she or he is excited or in a hurry. We clinicians have to note situations that tend to be particularly stressful. Determining the hierarchy of pressure situations continues to be an important aspect of traditional therapy.

Linguistic components consist of several possible disorders (1) of attending behaviour (2) of auditory processing in particular auditory sequential memory for linguistic units and (3) of language. Language disorders include disorders of semantics, syntax, morphology, pragmatics, or cognition.

Typical disorders are attending behaviour that you may observe in the child who stutters, or disorders of distraction behaviour (often associated with brain damaged individuals), hyperactivity and a general ability to attend to tasks.

Often competition between family members is a strong factor, especially for speaking situations. Some children apparently place themselves under excessive pressure to perform, perhaps as a result of subtle parental desires for them to achieve.

As a speech clinician, you must know the intra-personal components of the stuttering problems. Once obtained, you must consider the information and deal with it as with any other component of the disorder.

As you can see when considering the components of stuttering, when you begin to think about evaluating and treating the stutterer, the problem becomes more complex. So you need keep these factors in mind as you consider assessing and treating stutterers.

The hypnotist can infuse courage and self confidence in the children and the trouble of stammering can be eliminated by giving them hypnotic suggestions.

The hypnotist should first ascertain from the child or children who are considered to be suffering from stuttering. Generally the children cannot utter the sentences starting with the letters *a, aa, ka, ra, ya.*

After knowing full details about their difficulties connected with their trouble, you can put your patients into a trance and start your suggestions to them.

"You are feeling very very sleepy, very very sleepy, very very sleepy. From this moment you are rectifying your defect (of stuttering) in a permanent way. Till now you are unable to pronounce certain words.[+] From now on, you will be pronouncing those letters and words easily, very easily and you will be in future talking to anyone freely without any fear. You will be speaking fluently also. You are a healthy child. You are now going to change your stuttering habit permanently.[*] You are now able to pronounce the difficult letters and words easily.[•] Now speak aloud whatever you want to tell me. Or you can speak any dialogue or sing a song which you remember previously."

Let them speak for any length of time. They are in deep trance state and will be responding to your suggestions. You can record the proceedings on tape. When the hypnotic sleep is terminated, replay the recorded audio tape to them for their satisfaction. They will be regaining their self confidence.

You can train them in the art of self-hypnotism.

If they practise self-hypnotism as per your suggestions, they would be free from stuttering and they can lead their daily lives (not only in their homes but outside also i.e. in schools or at social gatherings etc.) with more self-confidence and to their satisfaction.

■■

+ Mention the words as per their case histories.

* If need be give suitable suggestions so as to put your subjects in deep trance state.

• Try to make arrangements to record the proceedings of the hypnotic session on audio tape.

Stage Hypnotism

The hypnotists have been giving stage shows from a very long time. The first hypnotist who had conducted such shows on scientific basis was Dr. Dean Coli of Bombay. In the year 1970 he paid a visit to Hyderabad and conducted Stage hypnotism shows for a period of eight days at Ravindra Bharathi under the auspices of Maharashtra Association. He had thus introduced the art of stage hypnotism to our Andhras. Till then I was conducting magic shows and he was aware of it. It was Dr. Dean Coli who advised me to conduct stage hypnotism shows also, which in fact naturally encouraged me. The next prominent hypnotist in our country is Dr. Bimani of Ahemedabad. Similarly, a mention may be made of Prof. Malayath, a magician and hypnotist of repute from Kerala State.

In 1952 a British Act of Parliament was passed which was devised to prevent as far as possible, such problems arising as were later anticipated by the MBA sub-committee. This is known as the Hypnotism Act 1952 and clause 2 (1) states - "No person shall give an exhibition demonstration or performance of hypnotism on any living person at or in connection with an entertainment to which the public are admitted whether on payment or otherwise unless the controlling authority have authorised that exhibition, demonstration or performance." For the benefit of readers, the Act is reproduced here.

British Hypnotism Act, 1952

A private member's Bill, introduced in 1952, became law the

same year. This Act was aimed at limiting the public exhibition of hypnotism as an entertainment. Unfortunately, since 1952 an increasing number of private clubs have been created for the purpose of entertainment plus drinking. Exhibitions given at such clubs are to members only and are thus not classified as "public" exhibitions. Stage hypnotism thus continues to flourish. The Hypnotism Act needs amendment before the police can act in these cases, and no doubt untold harm is done to the misguided individuals who volunteer and come up on the stage.

Doctors dealing with hypnosis should have knowledge of this Act. For permission to publish it, the author makes grateful acknowledgment to H.M. Stationery Officer as the owner of the copyright of the said Act. The contents including the clauses and provisions of the act are given below:

An Act to regulate the demonstrations of hypnotic phenomena for the purposes of public entertainment.   (1st August, 1952)

Be it enacted by the Queen's most Excellent Majesty, by and with the advice and consent of the Lords Spiritual and Temporal, and Commons, in this present Parliament assembled, and by the authority of the same as follows:

Control of demonstrations of hypnotism at places licensed for public entertainment.

1.1 Where under any enactment an authority in any area has power to grant licences for the regulation of places kept or ordinarily used for public dancing, singing, music or other public entertainment of the like kind, any power conferred by any enactment at attach conditions to any such licence shall include power to attach conditions regulating or prohibiting the giving of an exhibition, demonstration or performance of hypnotism on any person at the place to which the licence relates.

153

1.2 In the application of this section to Scotland, for the reference to places kept or ordinarily used for public dancing, singing, music or other public entertainment of the like kind there shall be substituted a reference to theatres or other places of public amusement or public entertainment.

Control of demonstrations of hypnotism at other places.

2.1 No person shall give any exhibition, demonstration or performance of hypnotism on any living person at or in connection with an entertainment to which the public are admitted, whether on payment or otherwise, at any place in relation to which such a licence as is mentioned in section one of this Act is not in force, unless the controlling authority have authorised that exhibition, demonstration or performance.

2.2 Any authorization under this section may be made subject to any conditions.

2.3 If a person gives an exhibition, demonstration or performance of hypnotism in contravention of this section, or in contravention of any conditions attached to an authorization under this section, he shall be liable on summary conviction to a fine not exceeding fifty pounds.

2.4 In this section, the expression "controlling authority" means

(a) in relation to a place in any such area as is mentioned in section one of this Act, the authority having power to grant licences of the kind mentioned in that section in that area;

(b) in relation to a place in any other area in England, the council of the country borough, borough, or urban or rural district where the place is, and in relation to a place in any other area in Scotland, the council of the country or burgh where the place is.

Prohibition on Hypnotising Persons Under Twenty-one

3. A person who gives an exhibition, demonstration or performance of hypnotism on a person who has not attained the age of twenty-one years at or in connection with an entertainment to which the public are admitted, whether on payment or otherwise, shall, unless he had reasonable cause to believe that that person had attained that age, be liable on summary conviction to a fine not exceeding fifty pounds.

Entry of Premises

4. Any police constable may enter any premises where any entertainment is held if he has reasonable cause to believe that any act is being or may be done in contravention of this Act.

Saving for Scientific Purposes

5. Nothing in this Act shall present the exhibition demonstration of performance of hypnotism (otherwise than at or in connection with an entertainment) for scientific or research purposes or for the treatment of mental or physical disease.

Interpretation

6. In this Act, except where the context otherwise requires it, the following expression shall have the meaning hereby assigned to it, that is to say: "hypnotism" includes hypnotism, mesmerism and any similar actor process which produces or is intended to produce in any person any form of induced sleep or trance in which the susceptibility of the mind of that person to suggestion or direction is increased or intended to be increased but does not include hypnotism, mesmerism or any such similar act or process which is self-induced.

Short Title, Extent and Commencement

7.1 This Act may be cited as the Hypnotism Act, 1952.

7.2 This Act shall not extend to Northern Ireland.

7.3 This Act shall come into force on the first day of April, nineteen hundred and fifty-three.

The hypnotist who aspires to give an exhibition or willing to conduct a stage hypnotic show should possess a good personality. If he himself is a fragile person and looks like a patient, the members of the audience cannot evince any interest in the show. The stage hypnotist should be well versed in the subject of hypnotism, his pronunciation and diction should be perfect. He should also possess a well modulated voice and should be a fluent speaker. Having neatly dressed and having a sufficient number of volunteers who have to assist him in the Stage Hypnotic Show as his subject, the hypnotist can begin the show according to his plans. The minimum number of audience should be around a hundred persons. Then only the show can be termed as a successful one in the general parlance.

The volunteers who are going to act as subjects at the particular show should be of the age group of 15 to 40 years. If a rehearsal of such would-be-subjects was conducted before the actual commencement of the show, it would be better not only to the hypnotist but also the members of the audience, to deem it as a successful one.

After sending your subjects into trance the following items can be conducted and the audience may find them with some amusement, happiness and some times observe them with exclamation!

1. Hand over a glass of water to one subject and give a suggestion to him that he is drinking sugar cane juice.

   After drinking the same, he would say "yes". Again hand over another glass of water to him and suggest that it is bitter. Tasting just a few drops of the same he would be returning the glass tumbler to you. He rejects to drink the same because he feels it is bitter as per your suggestions.

156

Stage Hypnotism — catalepsy

2. Give suggestions to some of your subjects, "You are not hearing any sounds, except my words, if any sound or any big sound is made here, such sound or sounds may not cause any disturbance to your sound sleep which you are now enjoying"—saying this, you ring a bell producing big sounds or disturbing sounds. Or throw a chair high into the air and let it fall on the floor of the place where you are conducting show, with a big bang. The members of the audience can hear the big bang or disturbing sounds which emanated from the bell. But the subjects who are under hypnotic trance would be enjoying their sleep to their heart's content (after this don't forget to cancel this suggestion).

3. Take one needle and clean it in hot water (sterilise the needle) now give a suggestion to one of your subjects as follows:— "Now I am going to count the numbers from 1 to 5. By the time I reach number 5 you will be losing the sense of touch of contact on your hand". Stating this you better inject the needle on his hand. Your subject would not express any symptom of pain and he would be feeling calm as if nothing happened.

157

4. A set of three chairs may be arranged on the floor and instruct one of your subjects to lie down on the three chairs. Give suggestions to your subject as follows:—"Now your body is getting a bit firm, hard, tight, and your body is now as stiff as a piece of wood. Now I am going to count the numbers from 1 to 5. By the time I reach number 5 your body will be as stiff as a piece of wood, Stating this, remove the middle chair. Your subject would be lying down on the two chairs as previously. Now you make a request among the members of the audience, a boy of lesser age (much younger than your Subject who is lying down on the two chairs) to come on to the stage and request him to stand on the stomach of the subject. The subject lying on the chairs would not feel any weight on his stomach even though the boy is actually standing on his stomach.

5. Give one carrot to some of your subjects to taste it and give suggestion to them if it is pungent. They would say "yes" or if you give a suggestion to them that it is sweet, they would be saying "yes".

6. Give a suggestion to one of your subjects who is in deep trance as follows: "Now your ability of smelling is greater, greater than ever. Now you can remember any smell correctly." You now collect three handkerchiefs from the members of the audience and put them one after another near the nose of your subject. State the numbers of the relevant handkerchief's as one, two and three respectively, to your subject to smell each handkerchief. Afterwards, you take one of the handkerchiefs, among them and again ask the subject to smell the same and ask him to state the exact number of the handkerchief on the basis of his smelling ability. The subject would be telling you the correct number of the handkerchief.

In the same manner you can conduct many experiments after some preparation and deft planning. If you plan new items for the purpose of your programme, naturally the audience can evince more interest in such programmes and this makes you happy and you would be elated when they praise you for arranging such a nice show.

Conclusion

The earlier chapters can train you as a good hypnotist. Even if you are not going to hypnotise others you can hypnotise yourself, find things easier to solve or overcome them, and, to made the changes which will give health, happiness and success to you.

I have devoured over many books on the subject, referred journals and cassettes and completed the book with my own experience in this field. But the science is unfathomable. Even then, I have mentioned the relevant information in a competent way.

The evolution of the use of hypnotism as an effective force for the treatment of various types of nervous illness and in certain specialised and clearly defined application, has added a powerful complimentary weapon to psychotherapy and psychiatry, as well as general practice, dentistry and many other disciplines of medicine and surgery.

Some of the recent findings indicate that not only mental and psychological diseases, but also some of the physical ailments can be cured by hypnotism. Further, the findings maintain that blood pressure can be controlled and gastric trouble can be contained and further advancement stopped. Some of the ailments which upset the health of the people because of "fear complex" can also be controlled by the efficacy of hypnotism.

The famous scientist J.B.S. Haldane gives some indication of the promise these techniques have for mankind in the following comment. "Any one who has seen even a single example of the power of hypnotism and suggestion, realises that the face of the world and the possibilities of existence will be totally altered when we can control their effects and standardise their applications, as has been possible for example, with drugs which were once regarded as equally magical".

The hypnotic and modern suggestion techniques are holding the same position today as penicillin and other antibiotics were a generation ago.

The self-hypnotic and self-suggestion techniques have been considered a turning point in the lives of many people not only in curing ailments but in overcoming the problems of every day life.

Hopefully, I have written sufficient to show that hypnosis has many applications and that although it is no panacea, it has considerable success in a variety of serious situations. Though there is as yet no single theory of hypnosis which is acceptable to all, the value of hypnosis as a therapy both alone and in combination with other methods of treatment are increasingly recognised.

We cannot change the past. Everyone of us will be having problems. The future is bright and we have to face it with mental calm, relaxation, concentration (controlled attention) and visualisation.

There is a thrill in life and for leading that life with contentment and happiness, the instrument is scientific hypnotism which is in your possession.

With the aid of this you can enrich your life and extend relief to other suffering multitude with a cool and sympathetic mind, mitigating their illness of mind and body and bring mental peace to the needy and succour to the society and to those who are near and dear to you.

Sarvejana Sukhino Bhavantu
May All Live in Happiness

■ ■

Explore the Power of Astrology—TRIKONA-2

—Dr. A.P. Sharma
Dr. V.K. Sharma

Dr Ambika Prasad Sharma and his son Dr Vinod Kumar Sharma, inspired by their two books on astrology, Explore the Power of Astrology and Explore the Power of Astrology Trikona One, bring to you a new and advanced viewpoint on another set of three important angles (houses) of the chart (kundali) which are the third house, the seventh house and the eleventh house, traditionally known as Trikona. These three houses deal with some of the crucial areas in one's life such as education, brothers and sisters, marriage, business partners, dreams and desires, gains through parents, and sudden and unexpected riches.

These findings combine both traditional Indian and Western viewpoints in the analysis of the charts. The authors have analysed over forty charts in relation to the three houses and discussed in detail how the planets play a vital role in the growth and development of human beings.

This book gives the reader an insight to unfold easily the hidden and overt impact of the planet(s) placed in a house and reflect extensively how these houses influence one's life constantly. It also provides the knowledge how the planets effect the houses they rule, and takes us a step further in unlocking and understanding the mysterious ways of the heavenly bodies.

Demy Size • Pages: 152
Price: Rs. 125/- • Postage: Rs. 15/-

PRACTICAL HYPNOTISM

—Dr. Narayan Dutt Shrimali

Towards the Quest of Awareness

In India, the art and science of hypnotism has been a priceless asset. It has been sanctified by timeless traditions. It was largely from India that the rest of the world learnt, followed and imbibed this knowledge.

Our ancient seers tried to discover the potential powers that lay embedded in the human body. They submitted themselves to the Almighty and went deep into the profound mysteries of the inner self.

On the other hand, the west was merely interested in exhibiting its deeds. It was more interested in showing off its superiority. The western idea, unmistakably was that man is what he himself wills to be. It also felt that man owes nothing whatsoever to the powers beyond, to the Creator and to the power of the soul.

Practical Hypnotism is a study, complete in all respects, which seeks to explain the science of hypnotism in simple, straight forward and unambiguous language. It makes an integrated study of the loftiest thoughts of the western thinkers and yet it heavily draws upon the priceless contemplations of the Indian seers of yore. For having achieved a fine blending of the two powerful strains of scholarship, the volume will commend itself to all strata of readership.

Demy Size • Pages: 236
Price: Rs. 96/- • Postage: Rs. 15/-

Instant Handwriting Analysis

—Ruth Gardner

Do your 'Gs' divulge a sensitive nature? Does your writing slant show you to be impulsive? Find out with Ruth Gardner's **Instant Handwriting Analysis.**

Handwriting patterns signal elements of your unconscious, and reveal your desires, fears, weaknesses, strengths, attitudes and more! With this book, someone who doesn't even know you could learn all about you in just a few moments!

This work covers some of the most important and basic factors of handwriting analysis for the explorer of Graphology — a scientific study on the field.

Now you can analyse your own handwriting and that of friends and family with this easy-to-use book. In just a few moments, you will know what the slant, stroke, word-spacing, margins, size and pressure, letter formations and signature reveal about your personality. You can even learn to change certain aspects of yourself by changing the way you write!

Compare your writing with the samples in this book — it's that simple! There is even a section on doodles. You may find that graphology is your next career or hobby!

Demy Size • Pages: 152
Price: Rs. 96/-• Postage: Rs. 15/-

Chakra & Kundalini WORKBOOK

—Dr. Jonn Mumford

For Physical and Spiritual Rejuvenation

The end of a millennium and the close of a century are always marked by tremendous social upheavals and radical political changes. Dr. Swami Gitananda stated in the 1950s that "it used to be the problems of man, now it is man, the problem!"

Chakra & Kundalini Workbook gives you remarkable psycho-physiological techniques to overcome the social and psychological chaos, inherent in the transition. It helps you build a solid experience of inner relaxation that will lead towards better health, a longer life and a greater control over your personal destiny.

The book is unique because it captures the best of the East and the West in a modern synthesis of purely efficient, concise and powerful "psychic" techniques combined with breath and posture.

The book:

❖ Provides a step-by-step guidance to the progressive Mind-Body exercises.

❖ Promotes better health and greater control over your personal destiny.

❖ Helps you in the attainment of an enriched Inner Life and Ultimate Enlightenment.

Demy Size • Pages: 264
Price: Rs. 110/- • Postage: Rs. 15/-

The Long Awaited Sequel to *How to Hypnotise Yourself & Others.* which has sold over 10,00,000 (ten lakh) copies!

Healing Power of Hypnotism

—*Rachel Copelan, Ph.D.*

Reach into your pockets and find the positive thinking that accompanies a stress-free lifestyle. Through Healing Power of Hypnotism, you will learn the most up-to-date, proven methods of hypnosis.

- ❖ Learn how to feel happy, release repressed anger and anxiety, heal, relieve stress, lose weight, sleep soundly, or want to run more, or lift weight.
- ❖ Learn the latest, tested methods of self-hypnosis.
- ❖ Learn to develop spiritually, psychically, mentally, physically and socially.

Group hypnosis dates back all the way to the Egyptians. Many ancient people performed group rituals which were hypnotic in nature. Mass chanting and hypnotic meditation to the steady beat of drums was widely accepted as part of the religious healing arts. Healing with the mind predates medical practice and is still used in many primitive societies.

Abolish Unhealthy Habits:
• Smoking • Over-eating • Insomnia • Caffeine-addiction

YOUR ABSOLUTE, QUINTESSENTIAL,
ALL YOU WANTED TO KNOW, COMPLETE GUIDE

Big Size • Pages: 264
Price: Rs. 150/- • Postage: Rs. 15/-

Horoscope Reading
Made Easy & Self-Learning

—*U.C. Mahajan*

Peep into your and your near
& dear one's future

Astrology by now is a tried and tested science, backed by centuries of analysis and interpretation. The planetary position in the individual charts, the causes and effects of specific conjunctions, the role of sun signs and ascendants—all the aspects of this discipline have been studied in depth by astrologers.

But for the reader, what makes the difference is the presentation of the material—and that's where this book scores over many others.

With a unique format by making extensive use of tables, point-by-point elucidation, explanatory notes and analysis, the book makes an interesting, easy and lucid readable volume. Backed by a thorough research of ancient astrology books of Urdu and English, the volume is a ready-reckoner for self-learners. What are the remedies for adverse star positions? What makes for long or short lines? How is marital bliss indicated in a particular chart? All this and whatever you're looking for is explained here in depth and detail. A must for every serious student of astrology.

Big Size • *Pages: 248*
Price: Rs. 150/- • *Postage: Rs. 15/-*

Richer Life Through Hypno Meditation

—Dr. Sanjoy Mukerji

A Journey to Prosperity, Self Development & Transformation

The indepth knowledge of human psychology, behavioural science and disorders, hypnosis, different types of meditation coupled with medical background led the author to develop 'Hypno Meditation', which is a unique amalgamation of western science and eastern wisdom. The technique of Hypno Meditation can help anyone gain access into the subconscious mind and harness the cybernetics. This practical handbook is a result of more than a decade of his intensive study, experience and research in the field of mind control.

The book tells all about:

❖ Mind ❖ Subconscious Mind ❖ Hypno Meditation (HM)

❖ Prosperity ❖ Money and Wealth

❖ Goal Setting and Success Principles

❖ Health and Stress ❖ Pain Control

❖ Result Sleep Induction ❖ Relationships

❖ Spiritual Growth ❖ General Guidelines

Demy Size • Pages: 107
Price: Rs. 80/- • Postage: Rs. 15/-